10 Perspectives on Innovation in Education

How do great educators bring about real change to make a difference in students' lives? In this first volume of the Routledge *Great Educators Series*, 10 of education's most inspiring thought-leaders come together to share their top suggestions you need right now to innovate in your school or classroom. You will gain fresh insights and practical strategies on these essential topics:

- Personalizing professional learning (Jeffrey Zoul)
- Promoting a positive school culture (Todd Whitaker)
- Improving our hiring practices (Jimmy Casas)
- Designing spaces that maximize learning (Thomas C. Murray)
- Empowering students in their learning and assessments (Starr Sackstein)
- Flipping the classroom to reach each student (Kirk Humphreys)
- Positioning libraries as learning hubs (Shannon McClintock Miller)
- Helping others embrace technology changes (Katrina Keene)
- Developing personal, not just professional, skills (Dwight Carter)
- Embracing each student's passions and strengths (LaVonna Roth)

Filled with inspiring stories throughout, the book will leave you feeling motivated to take risks and try new things in your own school or classroom. As the authors say, if we want to make a real difference, it's not enough to do the things we do better; we must also do new and better things!

Jimmy Casas (@casas_jimmy) is an educator, bestselling author, and speaker with 22 years of school leadership experience. He served 14 years as principal at Bettendorf High School in Bettendorf, Iowa. Under his leadership, Bettendorf was named one of the "Best High Schools" in the country three times by *Newsweek* and *US News & World Report*.

Todd Whitaker (@ToddWhitaker) is a professor of educational leadership at the University of Missouri. He is a leading presenter in the field of education and has written more than 50 books including the national bestsellers *What Great Teachers Do Differently* and *Your First Year: How to Survive and Thrive as a New Teacher,* co-written with Madeline Whitaker Good and Katherine Whitaker.

Jeffrey Zoul (@Jeff_Zoul) is a lifelong teacher, learner, and leader. During Jeff's distinguished career in education he has served in a variety of roles, most recently as assistant superintendent for teaching and learning with Deerfield Public Schools District 109 in Deerfield, Illinois. Jeff is president of ConnectEDD, an organization specializing in educational conferences, professional learning, consulting, and coaching.

10 Perspectives on Innovation in Education

Edited by Jimmy Casas, Todd Whitaker, and Jeffrey Zoul

Routledge
Taylor & Francis Group
NEW YORK AND LONDON

First published 2019
by Routledge
52 Vanderbilt Avenue, New York, NY 10017

and by Routledge
2 Park Square, Milton Park, Abingdon, Oxon, OX14 4RN

Routledge is an imprint of the Taylor & Francis Group, an informa business

Library of Congress Cataloging-in-Publication Data
Names: Casas, Jimmy, editor. | Whitaker, Todd, 1959– editor. |
Zoul, Jeffrey, editor.
Title: 10 perspectives on innovation in education /
edited by Jimmy Casas, Todd Whitaker, and Jeffrey Zoul.
Other titles: Ten perspectives on innovation in education
Description: New York : Routledge, 2019. |
Includes bibliographical references.
Identifiers: LCCN 2018041892 (print) | LCCN 2018052261 (ebook) |
ISBN 9780429486104 (ebook) | ISBN 9781138598829 (hardback) |
ISBN 9781138598836 (pbk.) | ISBN 9780429486104 (ebook)
Subjects: LCSH: Educational change. |
Educational innovations. | Teacher effectiveness.
Classification: LCC LB2805 (ebook) |
LCC LB2805 .A15 2019 (print) | DDC 371.2/07–dc23
LC record available at https://lccn.loc.gov/2018041892

ISBN: 978-1-138-59882-9 (hbk)
ISBN: 978-1-138-59883-6 (pbk)
ISBN: 978-0-429-48610-4 (ebk)

Typeset in Palatino
by Out of House Publishing

Contents

Meet the Authors

Jeffrey Zoul (@Jeff_Zoul) is a life-long teacher, learner, and leader. During Jeff's distinguished career in education he has served in a variety of roles, most recently as assistant superintendent for teaching and learning with Deerfield Public Schools District 109 in Deerfield, Illinois. Jeff also served as a teacher and coach in the state of Georgia for many years before moving into school administration. Jeff has also taught graduate courses at the uni-  versity level in the areas of assessment, research, and program evaluation. He is the author/co-author of many books, including *What Connected Educators Do Differently*, *Start. Right. Now. – Teach and Lead for Excellence*, *Improving Your School One Week at a Time*, and *Leading Professional Learning: Tools to Connect and Empower Teachers*. Jeff is president of ConnectEDD, an organization specializing in educational conferences, professional learning, consulting, and coaching. Jeff blogs at jeffreyzoul@blogspot.com

Todd Whitaker (@ToddWhitaker) has been fortunate to be able to blend his passion with his career. Prior to moving into higher education he was a math teacher and basketball coach in Missouri. Todd has written over 50 educational books including the bestsellers *What Great Teachers Do Differently* and *Your First Year: How to Survive and Thrive as a New Teacher* with Katherine Whitaker and Madeline Whitaker Good. Todd is married to Beth, also a former teacher and principal. They are both faculty members of educational leadership at the University of Missouri and professor emeritus at Indiana State University. They are the parents of three children: Katherine, Madeline, and Harrison.

Jimmy Casas (@casas_jimmy) has 22 years of school leadership experience at the secondary level. He received his BA in Spanish and Masters in Teaching from the University of Iowa, and his Masters in Administrative Leadership from Cardinal Stritch University in Milwaukee. Jimmy earned his superintendent endorsement from Drake University where he serves as an adjunct professor for Drake, teaching a graduate course on educational leadership. Jimmy served 14 years as principal at Bettendorf High School in Bettendorf, Iowa. His passion for teaching and learning coupled with a vision for developing a community of leaders procured a culture of excellence and high standards for learning amid a positive school culture for all students and staff. Under his leadership, Bettendorf was named one of the "Best High Schools" in the country three times by *Newsweek* and *US News & World Report*. Jimmy's core purpose lies in serving others. He continues to give back to his profession by speaking and presenting at the local, state, and national levels, and school districts around the country.

Thomas C. Murray (@thomasc murray) serves as the director of innovation for Future Ready Schools®, a project of the Alliance for Excellent Education, located in Washington, D.C. He has testified before the U.S. Congress and has worked alongside that body and the U.S. Senate, the White House, the U.S. Department of Education and state departments of education, corporations, and school districts throughout the country to imple-
ment student-centered, personalized learning while helping to lead Future Ready Schools® and Digital Learning Day. Murray serves as a regular conference keynote, was named the "2017 Education Thought Leader of the Year," and one of "20 to Watch" by the National School Boards Association, and the "Education Policy Person of the Year" by the Academy of Arts and Sciences in 2015. His bestselling book, *Learning Transformed: 8 Keys to Designing Tomorrow's Schools, Today*, was published by the Association for Supervision and Curriculum Development (ASCD) in 2017. Connect with him @thomascmurray or thomascmurray.com

Starr Sackstein (@mssackstein) has been an educator since 2001 and is currently director of humanities in the West Hempstead Union Free School district. Starr received national board certification in 2012 and was recognized as an outstanding educator that year by *Education Update*. She is also a certified Masters journalism educator through the Journalism Education Association (JEA) and served at the New York State Director to JEA. Most recently, she was named an ASCD "Emerging Leader" class of 2016 and had the opportunity to give a TEDx Talk called "A Recovering Perfectionist's Journey To Give Up Grades." She is author of *Teaching Mythology Exposed: Helping Teachers Create Visionary Classroom Perspective*, *Blogging for Educators*, *Teaching Students to Self Assess: How Do I Help Students Grow as Learners?*, *The Power of Questioning: Opening Up the World of Student Inquiry*, *Hacking Assessment: 10 Ways to Go Gradeless in a Traditional Grades School*, and *Empower Students to Give Feedback: Teaching Students to Provide Effective Peer Feedback*. She blogs on Education Week Teacher at "Work in Progress," co-moderates #sunchat and contributes to #NYedChat.

Kirk Humphreys (@Kirk_Humphreys) is a TAP math teacher at Caruso Middle School in Deerfield, Illinois. As an educator, Kirk prides himself in being an innovator and is constantly reinventing his math classroom. He has been the recipient of numerous awards which include the 2011 Illinois Air Force Association Teacher of the Year Award, the 2015 Illinois 10th District Exceptional Educator Leadership Award and is a Dispatch Master teacher.

Shannon McClintock Miller (@ shannonmmiller) currently serves as the K–12 teacher librarian at Van Meter Community School in Iowa and as the Future Ready Librarians spokesperson working with students, librarians, educators, and others around the world every day. She is Buncee's librarian advisor, Capstone's teacher librarian advocate and author, a Participate author and Skype educator. Shannon is the author of the award-winning The Library Voice

blog and enjoys writing for various blogs, journals, and other forums including the International Society for Technology in Education (ISTE), *School Library Journal*, and *Publishers Weekly*. She has published children's books about library skills with Capstone and is also writing a library leadership book with Bill Bass for ISTE. In 2014, Shannon was named "Library Journal Mover and Shaker." In 2016, she was awarded the Making it Happen Award by ISTE. In 2018, she was named the American Association of School Librarians "Social Media Superstar Leadership Luminary."

Katrina Keene (@DrKatrinaKeene) is a national and international speaker, and has spent the last 18 years in K–12+ technology education. Currently, Katrina is the senior strategic outreach manager in education at Wonder Workshop for the central U.S. Prior to this, Katrina was an education strategist for CDWG, director of technology, instructional technology coach, K-5 computer teacher, college professor, as well as a grade 3, grade 1,

and kindergarten teacher. Katrina loves staying connected with educators through Twitter, Instagram, Facebook,

Periscope, and other social media platforms and is thrilled to bring her expertise and research to thousands of schools across the nation. Katrina is an MIEExpert, Remind Connected Educator, founder of #tntechchat and #edcampleadtn, and can be found in several well-known EdTech publications, blogs, and podcasts.

Dwight Carter (@Dwight_Carter) was an award-winning principal in the Columbus, Ohio area. His focus has been and continues to be establishing positive relationships with stakeholders in order to do what is best for students. He has co-authored two books about learning spaces, understanding today's students, and leading schools in disruptive times. He recently began a new career as a leadership and effectiveness coach assisting school leaders and teachers to become more efficient and effective. He presents at a number of local, state, and national conferences about school leadership, school culture and climate, understanding today's students, and how to engage all stakeholders in a school community.

LaVonna Roth (@LaVonnaRoth) is lead illuminator, creator, and founder of Ignite Your S.H.I.N.E.® LaVonna challenges others to discover how to ignite the S.H.I.N.E. in their students, others, and self. Her mission is to help individuals discover who they are, what they can become, and to build self-motivation to see how far they can go. She will passionately stretch the status quo in education and invite you to join her so "shifts happen." As a highly energetic, dynamic, and engaging FUNnote (keynote) speaker, learning specialist, author and consultant, LaVonna has a BA in Special Education, a Masters in the Art of Teaching, and a Masters in Educational Leadership. She taught at the elementary and secondary levels and is the author of eight books. She has presented in the U.S., Canada, Europe, South America, and the Middle East on increasing engagement and the fun factor in learning. One way to get involved is through social media, using #igniteyourSHINE. Together, we got this!

About the *What Great Educators Do Differently* Conferences and the Routledge *Great Educators Series* Books

In 2015, Jeff Zoul, Jimmy Casas, and Todd Whitaker decided to organize a new type of professional learning conference for educators serving in any role, from classroom teacher to superintendent, and everything in between. They eventually created ConnectEDD (www.connectEDD.org) as an organization dedicated to inspiring and motivating educators everywhere to innovate, experiment, and connect with each other to become the very best they can be as professional educators. The first *What Great Educators Do Differently* conference was held in the Chicago area in the fall of 2015. Jeff, Jimmy, and Todd reached out to some of the best educators they knew and asked them to share their wisdom over the course of the two-day event. This inaugural conference was so successful, that they continued hosting events. Since that time, they have hosted ten additional events in seven different states as well as Canada.

At each conference, sessions are led by some of the world's most recognized and respected educators, including classroom teachers, principals, superintendents, librarians, instructional coaches, authors, technology specialists, and other educational leaders. *What Great Educators Do Differently* (WGEDD) conferences focus on topics most important to educators in schools today and emphasize connecting with each other during and after the conference to keep the learning moving forward. Everyone who presents at a WGEDD event works hard to make sure that attendees who are investing in their own professional learning by attending an event walk away not only re-energized and inspired about education and their role in the profession, but also with practical strategies for improving their work as educators. Conference participants connect with educators who share their passions, concerns, interests, challenges, goals, and commitments and are greeted with unparalleled professionalism and approachability from all WGEDD presenters throughout the conference – and even after the event.

What Great Educators Do Differently conferences represent the values and commitments of the event organizers and Routledge since its inception, including providing visionary presenters, opportunities for connecting among presenters and attendees, practical, strategies and tools, and ongoing crucial conversations.

Why a Book Series

Since the first WGEDD conference in 2015 to today, the feedback received from attendees has been overwhelmingly positive and gratifying. The number one response we hear from attendees as we shake the hand of each participant at the end of each event is simply this: "This is the best conference I have ever attended." After more than a dozen successful conferences, the idea for a series of books written by WGEDD speakers and based on WGEDD themes was hatched. Throughout the *What Great Educators Do Differently* journey, Routledge has sponsored many of the events and continues to support this work because of their passion for and commitment to ongoing professional improvement for all educators. When the idea for a book was born, Routledge was excited to partner with these educational authors to create a different kind of book; one we hope captures the spirit of actual WGEDD events.

Since its inception, over 50 esteemed educators have spoken at one or more WGEDD events, including the following:

◆ Todd Whitaker ◆ LaVonna Roth
◆ Jeff Zoul ◆ Pernille Ripp
◆ Jimmy Casas ◆ Katrina Keene
◆ Joe Sanfelippo ◆ Ross Cooper

- ◆ Brianna Hodges
- ◆ Thomas C. Murray
- ◆ George Couros
- ◆ Shannon Miller
- ◆ Sanee Bell
- ◆ Erin Klein
- ◆ Dwight Carter
- ◆ Derek McCoy
- ◆ Jennifer Hogan
- ◆ Amber Teamann
- ◆ Salome Thomas-El
- ◆ Kayla Delzer
- ◆ Brian Mendler
- ◆ Jessica Cabeen
- ◆ Ken Williams
- ◆ Marcie Faust
- ◆ Amy Fadeji
- ◆ Garnet Hillman
- ◆ Joe Mazza
- ◆ Katherine Whitaker
- ◆ Madeline Whitaker
- ◆ Kirk Humphreys
- ◆ Angela Maiers
- ◆ Paul Solarz
- ◆ Kim Hofmann
- ◆ Todd Nesloney
- ◆ Beth Houf
- ◆ Brad Gustafson
- ◆ Starr Sackstein
- ◆ Rafranz Davis
- ◆ John Trautwein
- ◆ Amy Fast
- ◆ A. J. Juliani
- ◆ Robert Dillon
- ◆ Trevor Greene
- ◆ Lisa Stevenson
- ◆ Weston Kieschnick

The idea for this new educational book series is to include the voices of each of these speakers in a one or more of the annual volumes. Each year, a new volume of the Routledge *Great Educators Series* will be published and will include the thoughts of ten or more educators/authors who have also presented at a *What Great Educators Do Differently* event. Each year the authors will write ten or more chapters that will be loosely focused on an overall theme to help educators continue their learning.

Launching the First Volume: All about Innovation

We begin the series, of course, with the volume you are reading. In this volume, we invited ten WGEDD speakers to weigh in on the theme of *Innovation in Education*. We are honored that the following educators agreed to support this book by contributing their thoughts on some aspect of education today and how we can become more innovative in how we think about and approach that part of our work as professional educators. Here, then, are the first ten authors in this new series:

Chapter 1: Jeffrey Zoul (@Jeff_Zoul): Jeff examines professional learning practices in our schools and makes a case for rethinking how we help our colleagues continuously grow and improve. He offers a framework for innovative professional learning practices which he calls, "The Six C's": *Choice, Connection, Context, Coaching, Curiosity,* and *Culture,* and explains how each is important in designing and delivering professional learning opportunities for educators. In addition, he shares and explains ten specific ideas for innovative professional learning ideas that are easily replicable in any school or district as a way to personalize learning for staff members.

Chapter 2: Todd Whitaker (@ToddWhitaker): Todd takes a look at the culture of our schools, our districts, and our classrooms. He maintains that school culture has an incredibly powerful influence on everything we do. Determining ways to continually move it in a positive direction is essential. These are truths. What we do with them is up to us. Although the ideas he shares here are not – according to him – necessarily "innovative," what makes them innovative is that we know we should do them but so many schools do not. Therefore, when we actually do these things to impact school, district, and classroom culture, we are innovating by trying something new and different.

Chapter 3: Jimmy Casas (@casas_jimmy): Jimmy suggests that we cannot accept status quo practices when it comes to selecting, recruiting, mentoring, and hiring new staff members. It is simply too important. He offers 12 steps for improving our hiring practices, including actions ranging from the interview process, to checking references, to making the offer to a new candidate. Hiring new staff members is simply one of the most important responsibilities of those already working within a school or district. We must be intentional about our hiring processes and practices. As Jimmy says, the more deposits we make throughout the hiring process, the greater the likelihood of a positive return on our investment and a win for our school community.

Chapter 4: Thomas C. Murray (@thomascmurray): Tom takes a deep-dive look into why learning spaces matter and how we can maximize student learning by intentionally designing the spaces in which teachers and students teach and learn. Tom examines many aspects of classroom learning environments and highlights what the research tells us about these. He cautions that we must remain hyperfocused on our why, and understand that simply placing new furniture and colorful beanbags into a space will not in and of itself improve student learning outcomes. It's the dynamic, innovative use of the learning space by the teacher and students that maximizes the impact on learning. Shifting pedagogy to focus on personal and authentic learning opportunities that leverage flexible and fluid spaces to maximize possibilities is ultimately the difference maker.

Chapter 5: Starr Sackstein (@mssackstein): Starr makes a strong case for involving students more actively in their own learning and offers a host of practical, specific ways to do so. She describes in great detail how to set up a student-centered learning environment, transparently embed standards throughout lessons, build student-designed learning experiences, determine success criteria collaboratively with students, release control of the learning to the learner, provide effective feedback, and promote a culture of reflection.

Chapter 6: Kirk Humphreys (@Kirk_Humphreys): Kirk provides an honest look at traditional math classrooms (including what his own looked like for many years), why they did not work for all students, and how we can do better. Too often when we think of a math classroom, we think of a classroom full of students facing forward and listening to their teaching explain the lesson for the day. If time permits, the teacher allows students to work on problems that are assigned. Any problems not completed by the end of class become homework. Students work through problems at home that mimic those in class. Students sometimes struggle at home on the homework, either not completing the homework or finding answers through friends or family. Students often wait until class the next day to ask questions about the problems they didn't understand on the homework. This pattern repeats itself throughout the school year. Math becomes a struggle for a lot of students. Kirk shares his practical ideas and strategies for changing the way students learn in a math classroom, taking authentic ownership of their own learning.

Chapter 7: Shannon McClintock Miller (@shannonmmiller): Shannon describes how our school libraries can become the true learning hubs of our school communities. Although everyone can play a role in transforming our school libraries into places of innovation, creativity, and collaboration, the transformation must begin with school librarians themselves. Shannon suggests five ways librarians can be true champions and leaders of innovation within their school communities and provides lots of practical strategies for becoming so.

Chapter 8: Katrina Keene (@DrKatrinaKeene): Katrina shares her own story about her life as an innovative educator and how her attempts at teaching outside the box were not always welcomed by her colleagues or administrators. Her practices were embraced, however, by those who mattered most – her students. So she continued to focus on innovation in each new role she had and working with others to help them innovate in their own school or classroom, but allowing each individual the freedom and autonomy to learn and grow in a way that worked best for them. Education as a whole is constantly inundated with new innovations, and in this chapter Katrina shares several ideas and theories on change while challenging both administrators and fellow educators to be patient with those who are slower to adopt new ideas, practices, and technologies.

Chapter 9: Dwight Carter (@Dwight_Carter): Dwight examines the importance of developing not just our "professional" skills, but also our "personal" skills. He explains why this is so important to the success of every classroom and every school. He shares his own frustrations and successes in developing his own personal skills as well as those around him. Dwight uses the "Be GREAT" acronym as a framework for focusing on personal skill development, suggesting that we should be: Grateful, Relational, Enthusiastic, Authentic, and Teachable. However, to be GREAT is more than just a catchy acronym. It is a way to focus our intentions on serving others in a way that influences their lives in a positive manner.

Chapter 10: LaVonna Roth (@LaVonnaRoth): LaVonna shares her vision for schools that embrace students' strengths and passions as a driving force in learning, that build up confidence on a daily basis, where students can experience career opportunities before they graduate so they are exposed to possibilities, and where ongoing experimentation and innovation are the norm. She challenges us all to make significant change happen to better serve every student in every school.

We hope you enjoy this first volume of the Routledge *Great Educators Series*. Please share your thoughts and contribute to the discussion on Twitter, using the #WGEDD hashtag. We are biased, of course, but we believe that education is the most important profession imaginable. What we do as educators matters, and it matters every day. We cannot afford to settle for the status quo in our work when we know a better way. When we know better, we must do better. Although we must always do the things we do better, we must also do new and better things in our classrooms, schools, and districts. Doing new and better things is how we innovate. Thank you for reading this book, sharing your thoughts – and innovating in your role as an educator.

1

Innovative Professional Learning

Jeffrey Zoul

An obvious characteristic of a successful school is that its students are learning at high levels. The more students learn, the better the school. Perhaps the best way to ensure that *students* are continuously learning and growing is to ensure that their *teachers* are also continuously learning and growing. There exists no greater variable impacting student learning than the quality of the classroom teacher. Schools get better when teachers get better. School leaders must embrace the responsibility of providing professional learning opportunities for all staff members designed to help them get better.

Unfortunately, in recent years, much has been written about traditional professional learning experiences suggesting these experiences result in little, if any, actual improvement. In fact, a 2013 report on professional learning by the National School Boards Association's Center for Public Education noted that most teachers are not provided the kind of professional development that would actually help them (1). Too often, the professional learning they receive arrives in the form of one-size-fits-all, one-time workshops. Even in the best of these instances, there is often little or no follow up or implementation in the classroom of what was "learned" in the workshop. The good news is that this is not necessarily a "time and money" problem which so often seems to be the lament of educators everywhere. Each year, $2.5 billion is spent on professional learning for educators at the federal level alone (2). In terms of time, we can always use more, of course, but every school and district in existence already dedicates a certain amount of time each school year to professional learning opportunities for its educators. Without increasing the money or time currently devoted to professional learning in our schools, we can do much better than the status quo. And we must. Our kids' learning depends on it; the time has come to invest in innovative professional learning experiences that respect adult learners.

Innovative Professional Learning Leads to Innovative Classroom Instruction

Somewhat ironically, it seems that we constantly hear about the need to innovate in terms of the instruction we provide students in our classrooms. Many teachers by now have likely sat through a workshop imploring them to become more innovative in the ways they teach their students. Unfortunately, most of these workshops have been delivered in decidedly non-innovative ways. If we want our teachers to innovate in their classrooms, they need to learn in innovative ways. Telling them to do it will not suffice; we must show them the way. Fortunately, I have witnessed several significant bright spots in districts around the country in terms of innovative professional learning practices, almost all of which are rather easily replicated. We can and should learn from these examples as a starting point for personalizing professional learning for educators just as we move to personalize learning for our students. It is important to note, however, that there is no single "best" way to provide learning for teachers any more than there is a single best way to design learning experiences for students. Moreover, not every type of professional learning experience we currently use needs to be eliminated from the menu of learning opportunities we provide staff members. Although I am a huge advocate for

> If we want our teachers to innovate in their classrooms, they need to learn in innovative ways.

student-centered learning in our classrooms, I also recognize the importance of whole group, direct instruction learning experiences and believe these should be incorporated into any innovative 21st century classroom. Similarly, there is nothing wrong with every staff member in a school district attending a keynote presentation in which the presenter simply shares his or her thoughts on how we can become better at what we do. The problem in both instances occurs when that is all we do or when we fail to follow up on the whole group instruction with targeted next steps and differentiated support for all learners. Not everything we are currently doing in our classrooms is bad. The same holds true for traditional professional learning. There are many things we should continue doing. At the same time, however, there are some things we should stop doing and many things we should start doing.

Two Frameworks for Thinking about Professional Learning

One thing we should start doing when planning professional learning is to adopt an overall framework and philosophy for the adult learning experiences we offer in our schools and districts. We should then develop our long-term professional learning plans with these overarching guiding principles in mind. Let me suggest two such frameworks. First, whenever I think about professional learning experiences for professional adults, I like to keep the work of Daniel Pink in mind; specifically, his thoughts on what motivates people to engage. Pink has written extensively about motivation (3), suggesting that the three key drivers of motivation are *Autonomy*, *Mastery*, and *Purpose*. Let's look at each briefly and how each might apply to professional learning for educators:

Autonomy: Autonomy is about giving people real control over various aspects of their work – including their professional learning. Pink recommends giving people autonomy over these four "T's": *Time, Team, Task, and Technique*. This

> We should strive to allow teachers a certain amount of choice in terms of when they will learn, with whom they will learn, how they will learn, and what they will learn.

is a powerful starting point for changing our approach to professional learning in our schools and districts: When designing innovative professional learning opportunities, we should strive to allow teachers a certain amount of choice in terms of *when* they will learn, *with whom* they will learn, *how* they will learn, and *what* they will learn.

Mastery: A sense of progress, in our work and in our capabilities, contributes to our inner drive. When designing professional learning experiences for educators, we must calibrate what people *must do* by looking at what they *can do*. If the must-do tasks are too difficult, people will become worried, frustrated, and feel out of their league. If the must-do tasks are too easy, they will get bored and disengage. Making progress in meaningful work is the single greatest motivator of human beings, according to Pink. When designing innovative professional learning opportunities, we should strive to design experiences that are meaningful to the learner and which challenge them to get better while also taking into account their current level of capacity.

Purpose: People can be inspired to meet stretch goals and tackle impossible challenges if they care about the outcome and if that outcome is something much bigger than themselves. All schools and districts face their own unique rollercoaster of ups and downs during the course of every school year. True purpose in the work allows these swings to create less distraction for educators on the team. When designing innovative professional learning opportunities, we should strive to connect the learning to something larger than teachers themselves. Although data are important, we must move beyond mere measurement, connecting these numbers and figures to people – most importantly, to students – and to values. We must strive to help those we serve view their work as not merely making a contribution, but making a difference.

A second framework for designing innovative professional learning experiences for educators is one I created using the 4 "C's" of 21st century learning as a starting point. In fact, these 4 C's have evolved into the 6 C's (4): *Communication, Collaboration, Creativity, Critical Thinking, Citizenship,* and *Character Education.* When designing professional learning experiences, I suggest we focus on "The Six C's" of Innovative Professional Learning and keep these in mind as we try to become more innovative: *Choice, Connection, Context, Coaching, Curiosity,* and *Culture.* Let's look at each briefly, examining how each might apply to professional learning for educators:

Choice: This is directly related to Pink's focus on autonomy, but stated simply, teachers should have a certain amount of choice about what they learn, when they learn, how they learn, and with whom they learn. In recent years, we have heard quite a bit about student voice and student choice, investing in their perspectives when designing learning experiences. We need to push just as passionately for raising teacher voice and teacher choice when it comes to professional learning. A good starting point when designing innovative professional learning experiences is empowering teachers to own their learning. Choice is one way to accomplish that goal.

Connection: Teachers need to connect with other teachers, in particular, teachers who share their professional passions, interests, responsibilities, and goals. Although I have written extensively about the importance of connecting with educators around the world (5), connecting with others to grow professionally is more than merely connecting through social media outlets. Teachers also need to connect in person, within their own school on teams, grade levels, and departments of which they are members. They need to connect with colleagues at other schools in their district and teachers in neighboring districts. When teachers connect with teachers, they learn new ideas and perspectives from people who are facing similar challenges and experimenting with new and different

> Innovative professional learning rarely, if ever, happens in isolation. There must be some aspect of professional discourse which moves beyond mere collegiality and into meaningful connections.

solutions to achieving better results. Innovative professional learning rarely, if ever, happens in isolation. There must be some aspect of professional discourse which moves beyond mere collegiality and into meaningful connections.

Context: Just as we seldom learn when we are isolated from other professionals, we are also less likely to experience authentic learning when what we are learning is isolated from any practical context. Once again, what holds true in the classroom for our students holds true for us as adult learners. In the classroom, learning facts and knowledge about a topic may well be an important prerequisite to understanding that topic and then developing mastery of and expertise with the topic. The key to gaining this true understanding and expertise, however, is providing a *context* for the information students (of all ages, including educators themselves) learn. The context becomes the glue to connect the dots along the path to applying the learning in real-world settings – such as our classrooms. Innovative professional learning requires context; authentic and relevant settings in which educators not only *know* something, but *do* something with what they know.

Coaching: The most-read blog post I have written in the past several years is a short piece I titled, *Teaching Should Be More Like Coaching* (6), in which I make the case that our students will grow more and truly acquire more knowledge and skills if we coach them to proficiency as opposed to teaching them to proficiency. When it comes to professional learning, we need to *coach* our teachers, not just *teach* our teachers. Coaching includes allowing time for the practicing of new skills, offering frequent, but brief, "mini-lessons" about new teaching techniques, circling back to previous learning and increasing complexity of the learning when we do, and, most importantly, providing feedback based on observation, letting teachers know what we have noticed and brainstorming together possible next steps for improvement.

Innovative professional learning includes opportunities for educators to coach and mentor each other. These roles need not be static, either: the teacher who coaches one day can be the mentee the next.

Curiosity: One of the most important components to learning – at any age – is the actual desire to learn. In our classrooms, we need to cultivate curious students. In our professional learning endeavors, we also must strive to instill curiosity within our adult learners. Albert Einstein once suggested about his own learning, "I have no special talents; I am only passionately curious" (7). Teachers who are passionately curious are far more likely to discover new and better ways to solve problems we face in our profession. How do we cultivate curiosity in our teachers? We can start by being openly curious ourselves, asking teachers for whom we are designing professional learning questions about their content, their instructional techniques, their challenges, their successes, why they think as they do, and any number of honest queries to which we would welcome their insights. We can also encourage curiosity by allowing teachers more freedom in their own learning, providing them space to explore, wonder, and ask questions. Carving out specific time for wondering will affirm teachers in their desire to learn. Innovative professional learning requires curious learners – which will only happen when they are supported by curious leaders who invite questions and encourage exploration of new ideas and thinking.

Culture: Without the proper culture in place, we need not worry about the preceding 5 C's because they are unlikely to occur. School leaders must work together to create a culture of curiosity, connection, and choice. They must work together to ensure the culture promotes learning in context and allows for coaching among all staff members. The culture within a district and school largely determines the amount of professional learning and growth that will occur. Innovative professional

> The culture within a district and school largely determines the amount of professional learning and growth that will occur.

learning requires an innovative culture; one in which commonly shared values are explicit and adhered to, one in which risk taking is encouraged and celebrated, one in which transparency and vulnerability are the norm rather than the exception, one in which hopes and dreams are fed rather than squashed, and one in which all adults in the organization know that the more they grow and learn, the more their students will grow and learn.

10 Ways to Design and Deliver Innovative Professional Learning

Now that we have established a working framework for what undergirds innovative professional learning, let us take a look at ten practical, specific ideas for designing and implementing innovative professional learning experiences. The following list includes ideas I have either implemented myself in schools and districts at which I have served or seen other school leaders implement in person when visiting schools. These ideas take into account one or more aspects of Pink's theory about what motivates us and my own belief about the importance of "The Six C's" of Innovative Professional Learning.

Twitter Chats

My guess is that most people reading this book have participated in at least one Twitter chat for educational purposes. Although I suspect my hunch is correct, we also must remember that the vast majority of staff members in the vast majority of schools *have not* participated in a Twitter chat. Moreover, they likely never will if left to their own devices. We can remedy that by scheduling Twitter chats into a professional learning day. The worst case result of doing so is that every single staff member will now have participated in one version of a Twitter chat. The best case scenario is that after doing so, at least some teachers will now have their curiosity piqued, will have learned something, and will continue to participate in similar chats on their own time to learn even more.

One way to do this: There are infinite ways to incorporate Twitter chats as part of an overall professional learning plan. Here is one way we accomplished this at a district in which I served: During a full day that was set aside for professional learning, we had a number of important items to accomplish. Different teachers would be attending different sessions throughout the day, depending on their role and/or school assignment. We ensured that regardless of role and school, each person would have some time during the day in which they could participate in a brief Twitter chat. We called on 12 staff members across the district who were already comfortable moderating a Twitter chat and assigned two each to six different time slots to co-moderate a chat. The chats were scheduled at six different times throughout the day, with each lasting for 20 minutes and including three questions about a teaching and learning topic that was important in our district at the time. Every staff member was asked to choose one chat in which to participate during the day and we ensured that each staff member had at least two time slots among the six when they had no other assigned responsibilities. We chose three different topics and repeated each topic twice to increase the chances that every staff member could participate in a topic of their choosing.

At the end of the day, every staff member in the district – including central office staff, principals, classroom teachers, social workers, speech language pathologists, and paraprofessionals – participated in a Twitter chat. Although we had been encouraging staff members to participate in Twitter chats outside of school, explaining how to do so as well as the benefits of doing so, this was the first time we actually provided time during contractual hours to ensure that everyone actually had the opportunity to participate. Most staff members in the district moved from "knowing" about Twitter chats to "doing" a Twitter chat. Feedback afterwards was largely positive, with many folks stating that they had always wanted to participate in a chat but never had time in the evenings or on weekends. Of course, for many staff members, this was the one and only time they participated in a chat, but even in these cases, people seemed to enjoy the experience and could see the benefit of discussing important topics with other educators.

Teachers Observing Teachers

This may not seem like an "innovative" professional learning idea, but based on my experiences in a long career in education, serving in many schools in many states, teaching remains a largely isolated profession. Despite valiant attempts at collaboration and a significant amount of collegiality, once the morning bell rings, we all seem to go to our respective spaces and get to work with "our" kids without ever observing a colleague or ever having a colleague observe us. As educators, one of the best ways we can learn new techniques is by observing other educators who are doing the same work we do. This need not be limited to classroom teachers, either. Though I am a strong proponent of allowing – even requiring – classroom teachers to observe each other teaching, it is equally important for administrators to observe each other. Whenever we do this, it is imperative that such visits are non-judgmental and non-evaluative. These visits should be validating for both the observer and the "observee." I have facilitated and participated in numerous individual and team observations of this type and they have always proved worthwhile for everyone involved. A common reflection I hear afterwards is something along the lines of, "You know, getting to see several of my colleagues in action actually validated what I was doing in my own classroom. At the same time, I learned a few new things I had never thought of before and I am going to try out these ideas in my classroom."

One way to do this: There are endless ways to incorporate peer observations as part of an overall professional learning plan. Many school districts have incorporated "instructional rounds" (8) into their schools, following the framework described by City et al., or modifying the practice to better suit their unique goals. Having teams of educators visit a school and conduct a series of brief visits to many classrooms throughout the day and then reflecting on the day while providing feedback to the school at which they observed is something I highly recommend. Here is another simple way we accomplished the goal of individual teachers observing their colleagues throughout the year at one school: Our middle school initials were "OMS" and we created a peer observation concept using the school initials to represent "Observing Masterful Staff."

Each month, every staff member completed one peer observation that lasted for 15 minutes. After the visit, the observing teacher would provide simple feedback to the colleague s/he observed listed under two categories: "Wows" and "Wonders." At first, some teachers were a bit apprehensive about this practice, but it soon became part of the culture at the school and an authentic way for teachers to validate – and learn from – each other.

School and District Edcamps

Similar to Twitter chats, we may not be able to bring every educator in our school or district to the edcamp, but we can bring the edcamp to every educator in our school or district. Edcamps are another authentic way to engage professional educators in meaningful conversations about topics important to them.

One way to do this: There are many ways to include edcamp-style learning as part of an overall professional learning plan. Here is one way we accomplished this at a district in which I served: During a regularly scheduled half-day of professional learning, we decided to use the entire time to conduct our own edcamp. The idea was relatively new at the time, and about a dozen folks in the district had attended an official edcamp and returned enthused, so we decided to schedule our own version. There were approximately 400 staff members in the district, so we scheduled 20 different topics from which people could choose to attend during three different time slots, with each lasting 30 minutes. Prior to the afternoon, we sent out a number of communications to all staff in an attempt to explain ahead of time what the idea behind an edcamp is and how our version would work. We needed a lot of sessions (60) and were a bit nervous that staff members would be reluctant to step up and pitch an idea for a session so, prior to the date, we actually asked several folks who had attended edcamps to be among the first to come to the microphone and share a session topic. As it turned out, this was unnecessary; we had dozens of staff members eagerly step up, sharing an idea for a session. We started the afternoon with a 30-minute time block to remind everyone of the structure and to build the schedule for the day's professional conversations.

Then, each staff member chose three different sessions to attend for the remainder of the afternoon. Feedback for the afternoon edcamp was as positive as any we had received for any previous professional learning event we held and several schools subsequently incorporated edcamp-style learning into their school-based professional learning time.

Student-Led Professional Learning

I served as a classroom teacher for 18 years. During these years, some of the people I learned the most from when it came to informing my own practice were my fellow teachers. The other people who taught me the most about how to be a good teacher? My students. The very best educators I know today are people who genuinely care about listening to, and learning from, the students they serve. In recent years, with the advent of technology in our homes and classrooms, many students come to our classrooms knowing more about technology than we do. That can be intimidating – or a wonderful source for learning and getting better. Although we need not limit how and what we learn from our students to technology, learning about their tech skills and needs is often a good entry point. It is also an easy way to honor our students by asking them what they know, what they can teach us, and how we can use their ideas to help them even more.

> The very best educators I know today are people who genuinely care about listening to, and learning from, the students they serve.

One way to do this: There are infinite ways to incorporate student-led learning as part of an overall professional learning plan. Here is one way school leaders accomplished this at a school I visited: Prior to the event, the principal set the context for the upcoming student-led professional development workshops by connecting what students and staff members would be doing to the district mission, which included high levels of learning for *all* learners (including teachers). This was an opportunity for students to become teachers and teachers to become students in a fun and meaningful way. The students (who were in grades 5–8) designed mini-workshops on a variety of tech topics, including

Google tools, social media, educational gaming tools, iMovies, and website design, along with any number of apps. The sessions ran for 20 minutes and each teacher attended two sessions. These were incorporated into a regularly scheduled "faculty meeting" time at the school. The school organizers tapped into areas about which their kids were excited and felt like experts. Since students are digital natives and have experiences with technology that we may not, having them lead professional learning about tech tools seemed a natural starting point in terms of students teaching teachers. At this school, the students simply agreed to meet after school as a group to work on their presentations, though they were also allowed time in class to do a trial presentation in front of their classmates. These students (like students everywhere) proved to be amazing facilitators of learning when given the opportunity to teach.

Collaborative Writing Projects

In the summer of 2017, I met in Philadelphia with nine other educators for the inaugural #EdWriteNow project, a 48-hour event in which those of us gathered wrote a full-length book (9). This collaborative project was a challenging, fun, and rewarding experience; everyone left having contributed to the project while learning just a little bit more about their fellow contributors as well as specific issues in education. Afterwards, I was approached by several individuals and groups around the country who wanted to host a similar event. The more I discussed this with other people, the more I realized that this could also be an authentic and productive professional learning experience for educators at any school or district. As a former English teacher, I often stressed the importance of not only *learning to write*, but also *writing to learn*. Writing about any topic can be an excellent way to learn about that topic and the learning is enhanced when the writing project becomes collaborative, rather than merely individual.

One way to do this: There are infinite ways to incorporate professional writing into an overall professional learning plan. Here is one way: Each summer, the district held its annual leadership retreat for all school administrators in the district. This was typically a three-day event during which school leaders from across the district gathered to reflect on the previous school year and plan for the upcoming one. Each year, the format remained pretty much the same, but the superintendent decided to change things for the most recent retreat, devoting one of the retreat days to writing. They set the stage for the "writing retreat" within the leadership retreat well in advance so that each administrator could spend the entire day simply writing. The goal for each individual was to write a "chapter" between 2,000–4,000 words in length that highlighted an effective teaching practice they had observed at their respective schools the previous year. The superintendent asked everyone to describe the technique, why it was effective, how it worked in practice, and how it could be adapted to other schools, grade levels, and content areas. This was a fairly small district, with approximately 35 total administrators. At the end of a single day, they had produced an 80,000 word document filled with actual teaching techniques that worked. Although they did not plan on publishing the book commercially, they did create a professional-looking text that became available to all staff members in the district as a resource. Although this example was done for school administrators, it could easily be produced by all staff members at an individual school, a team of instructional coaches in a school district, or almost any other group of educators who want to gather together to share their insights through a collaborative writing project.

Genius Time

Much has been written in recent years about how Google and other companies allow a certain amount of time for employees to simply explore and work on projects of their own choosing. This concept has been adapted into many classrooms, with teachers allowing students to work on projects about which they are passionate. The names and structures for such classroom programs vary, but, in essence, they are all designed to allow students to explore their own interests and encourage creativity in the classroom. They provide students with a choice in what they learn and how they will demonstrate their learning during a set period of time in school. As is often the case, what works for student learning can also apply to teacher learning. Any innovative professional learning plan should incorporate a certain amount of

"Genius Time," in which staff members choose what to work on and how to share what they have learned through this time.

One way to do this: There are infinite ways to incorporate Genius Time into an overall professional learning plan. Here is one way school leaders accomplished this: The overall framework for the district's teacher Genius Time plan was captured with the acronym, DQ RISE, which represented the five components of their Genius Time plan:

Driving Question: Each staff member in the district came up with a topic about which they wanted to learn that related to their specific role. They created a driving question about the topic which would "drive" their learning during this time. Almost any topic was acceptable within the guidelines that it should be: 1. Something that would benefit students, staff, or the school as a whole; 2. Driven by the individual's interests and passion; and 3. An area of "new" learning for the staff member, not something they had already "learned."

Research: Each staff member would then "research" their topic of interest. Of course, this research could take many forms in addition to traditional research methods. Staff members would keep track of the hours they spent on this part of the process since the district required a certain amount of hours to be devoted to this learning. Some of the hours occurred on the teacher's own time, but the district also set aside time within contractual hours for teachers to pursue their Genius Time learning/research.

Implement: Staff members were expected to implement something new and different in their classroom (or in some other setting, depending on their role) as a result of the research they were conducting about their topic. For some, the implementation was an ongoing event; in other instances, the implementation came at one point in time. This depended on the individual project and the person's role in the district.

Share: Each staff member was expected to share the results of their Genius Time learning, but how they shared this learning was largely up to each individual and could be quite formal or very informal. There was a form to complete as well as a meeting with an evaluator/supervisor to reflect on what they learned, what went well, what they might do differently upon reflection, and any other next steps.

Evaluate: For this stage of the process, the district simply sought feedback from each participant about whether they thought the program was meaningful, how it could be improved, and to what extent their Genius Time made a difference in their professional life during the school year.

Staff Field Trips

We can learn a great deal from the colleagues with whom we serve in our own school. We can also learn from colleagues in other schools within our own district. One often-overlooked way to learn from other educators is by making site visits to other districts, schools, and classrooms to see how they are addressing the same issues we are facing in our home district. Innovative professional learning plans include time for educators to observe and converse with educators in other districts.

One way to do this: There are many ways to incorporate site visits into an overall professional learning plan. Here is how Jimmy Casas accomplished this with his team when he was principal at Bettendorf High School in Iowa: Jimmy and his team took the idea of site visits to a completely new level, transforming these events into actual teacher exchanges. On more than one occasion, Jimmy and a team of Bettendorf High School teachers took a road trip to visit a high school in another state. Bettendorf team members spent the night in homes of host school staff members, then spent the following day shadowing that staff member at their school. Subsequent to this visit, the Bettendorf team repaid the favor, inviting staff members from their exchange high school to spend the night in their homes and then observe in their classrooms. Obviously, there are easier ways to conduct site visits by simply spending a day or half-day visiting a school in a neighboring district, but having staff members spend the night and entire day with educators in an entirely different state is an innovative way to connect and learn from educators further away who may have much to offer.

Speed Dating

In recent years, I have participated in several different versions of professional learning activities based on the concept of "speed dating." Although the format of these activities has varied widely, the general idea is to share many great ideas in a short amount of time. When implemented in schools or districts, a typical version of speed dating professional learning involves a number of staff members who are willing to share an idea they are using successfully with colleagues who rotate from individual to individual or from group to group. Although the content shared at each station can be about anything, I have often seen this idea used to quickly share information about tech tools and apps.

One way to do this: There are endless ways to incorporate speed dating into an overall professional learning plan. Here is one way school leaders can design this activity: In place of a regular staff meeting, schedule a "speed dating" staff meeting. A relatively simple way to schedule this is to call on a number of teachers to prepare and deliver a 5–10-minute session on any topic. The number of sessions needed may depend on the number of staff members in the school. If there are 100 staff members, you might ask seven different staff members to lead a session that would last for seven minutes and which they would repeat seven times. Have each of the seven sessions take place in adjoining classrooms and randomly assign approximately 15 staff members into seven different groups. These groups would then rotate to all seven sessions. With a two-minute break in between, the entire activity would only require about an hour of time and every staff member would have the opportunity to learn about seven new ideas.

TED-Style Talks

TED Talks began in Monterey, California in 2006 and have since skyrocketed in popularity (10). Traditional TED Talks are presentations in which the presenter shares an idea in 18 minutes or less. At two middle schools in Deerfield, Illinois, teachers decided to incorporate this idea as a creative way for students to demonstrate mastery of several Common Core English language arts standards. These proved to be hugely successful projects which required students to conduct research, write, and speak effect-ively. After observing students delivering their TED Talks on a wide variety of topics, I suggested that this might be something we invite teachers to do, too, as part of their professional learning. The idea was to simply mirror the TED Talk idea, with staff members choosing a topic of passion and/or expertise and sharing their idea with their colleagues in a talk lasting 18 minutes or less.

One way to do this: There are a number of ways to incorporate TED Talks into an overall professional learning plan. Here is one way school leaders designed this activity at one of the middle schools in the Deerfield district: Rather than ask individual teachers to plan and deliver a TED Talk, the principal decided to have each team of teachers collaborate on this task, working together to plan the talk, with each team member presenting a portion of the 18-minute talk. The principal believed that this would be a less intimidating way to approach this new idea rather than asking individuals to step up and deliver a talk. He asked every team at the school (e.g., grade 6, PE, Student Services) to participate and provided time to prepare during professional learning blocks of time. His only guidance in terms of content was to ask each team to share with their colleagues some practice(s) they had implemented that were having a positive impact on student per-formance. On the day of the presentations, I visited the school to observe and was impressed with what information was shared by each team and how they shared it. *A final note:* In an effort to model the technique, the school's administration team was the first team to present. School leaders cannot ask teachers to try new ideas if they are not willing to participate themselves.

Badging/Credentialing

Too often in professional learning we focus too much on the plan we have in mind for the learning and not enough on what teachers already know and can do, and how much support they will – or will not – need to master new learning. Rather than requiring all staff

> Too often in professional learning we focus too much on the plan we have in mind for the learning and not enough on what teachers already know and can do, and how much support they will – or will not – need to master new learning.

members to sit through the same workshops, why not design anytime, anywhere learning experiences that teachers can tackle, learning new information and/or skills and then doing something with the learning to demonstrate mastery? Once they do, we can provide them with a badge (digital or actual) or credential that represents their proficiency in a given area. Currently, traditional credentials for students and teachers are the diplomas they receive at various stages along their academic journeys. At the college level, these credentials are time consuming and expensive. Moreover, they are a bit vague in terms of describing what, exactly, the owner of the diploma actually knows and is able to do. What is truly important is not the diploma itself, but what the owner of the diploma can do as a result. The fact that we possess a diploma is, ultimately, unimportant. What truly matters is whether we can perform the required skills necessary to succeed. If one can perform the skills, the diploma is subordinate in importance – possibly even irrelevant – and could actually come from an alternative source of credentialing (the school or district in which the teacher works) rather than the typical source (a college or university). What if school districts designed specific credential opportunities for a wide variety of skills and allowed any staff member to attempt to earn these credentials anytime and anywhere as a way to better themselves? What if teachers were even allowed to advance their pay level by proving they had acquired new knowledge and skills, instead of putting in the required seat time and credit hours to earn another diploma? Speaking only for myself and reflecting on my Masters, specialist's, and Doctoral degrees, I think such learning might have been more efficient, cost effective, and relevant than most of the traditional graduate-level education courses I endured. Allowing teachers to earn badges or credentials for new skills they have acquired can be an innovative way to recognize them for growing professionally.

One way to do this: There are limitless ways to incorporate badging/credentialing opportunities as part of an overall professional learning plan. This example is another one we created when I served as assistant superintendent in Deerfield, Illinois: Our foray into credentialing began with a professional learning platform we called, "Deerfield University." This platform allowed staff members to earn badges and incentive points on a voluntary basis by learning about a topic, doing something with their learning, and submitting evidence of their application of learning. We began by identifying five areas of learning that were critical to the district and called these five areas "campuses" within the "university." For us, the five campuses included: 1. Tech Tools, 2. Standards-Based Grading and Assessment, 3. Social–Emotional Learning, 4. Project-Based Learning, and 5. Standards-Based Unit Design. Within each campus, we designed six courses teachers could choose to attempt. For each course, we identified the key knowledge and skills we wanted our staff members to possess and then determined methods for measuring mastery of this. Although every course was unique, our goal was to have the "learning" component of each take no more than an hour. In addition, each course had a "doing" component which varied in terms of time commitment. Once we created the 30 total course offerings, we launched the concept during a scheduled professional learning day. For that day, we created a special course that could be accomplished during the day so every staff member in the district earned at least one Deerfield University badge. Afterwards, the program was strictly voluntary, with teachers simply choosing whether to participate. We did include small incentives along the way, including whenever a staff member successfully completed all six courses within a single campus, and a significant prize for any staff member who completed all 30 courses, thereby becoming "graduates" of Deerfield University. Although the program was voluntary, we were pleased with the participation, with more than half of all staff members earning five or more badges and seven staff members earning badges for all 30 courses during the first year.

Making It Personal; Making It Work

The above ten examples describing innovative professional learning experiences for educators merely scratch the surface of possibilities – including many other excellent ideas that are already in place at schools and districts around the world. What makes each of these ideas innovative is simply the fact that they take into account Pink's theory of motivation and incorporate one or more of "The Six C's" of Innovative Professional Learning. Although each is important, perhaps the most important is *choice*/autonomy. Fortunately, allowing teachers choice in what, how, when, and with whom they learn is something that may also be the easiest C to address. We simply need to make it happen. Anyone who has studied the idea of "professional learning communities" (11) knows that two questions we must continuously ask ourselves when designing instruction and analyzing assessments include: 1. What is it we want all students to know and be able to do? and 2. How will we know if they know it? District and school administrators may well ask these same two questions, with a slight twist, of every teacher when planning professional learning experiences: 1. What is it we want all staff members to know and be able to do? and 2. How will we know if they have learned it? It will always be fair and appropriate to expect that all staff members in a school or district learn specific new skills necessary to successfully implement school and district initiatives and fulfill the school and district mission. We need not eliminate all traditional professional learning goals, formats, or beliefs that are currently in place. However, we must also look at more innovative ways to prepare, motivate, and grow the colleagues we serve. When trying to innovate, a simple starting point is to make a slight shift on these two questions and also ask each teacher in our district or school: 1. What is something new *you* want to learn and be able to do professionally? and 2. How will *you* show us what you learned once you've learned it?

In short, we need to do for teachers what we so often ask teachers to do for their students: personalize learning. There are many ways to define "personalized

> We need to do for teachers what we so often ask teachers to do for their students: personalize learning.

learning" for students. Perhaps my favorite is a definition from folks at the Gates Foundation (12) – by changing just a few words (that I have taken the liberty to add in parentheses), we also have a working definition of personalized learning for professionals:

> Personalized learning seeks to accelerate student (teacher) learning by tailoring the instructional environment – what, when, how, and where students (teachers) learn – to address the individual needs, skills, and interests of each student (teacher). Students (Teachers) can take ownership of their own learning, while also developing deep, personal connections with each other, their teachers (colleagues) and other adults (in their Personal Learning Network).

To become more innovative in our classrooms, we must become more innovative in the way we design learning for teachers. We can do this. We must do this. Let's make it personal.

References

1. Teaching the Teachers: Effective Professional Development. (2013, September 1). Retrieved June 1, 2018, from www.centerforpubliceducation.org/research/teaching-teachers-effective-professional-development
2. Strauss, V. (2014, March 1). Why Most Professional Development for Teachers is Useless. Retrieved June 1, 2018, from www.washingtonpost.com/news/answer-sheet/wp/2014/03/01/why-most-professional-development-for-teachers-is-useless/?noredirect=on&utm_term=.96a2072bee6f
3. Pink, D. H. (2009). *Drive*. New York: Riverhead Books.
4. Knezevic, D. (2018, January 12). 21st Century Skills: 6 C's of Education in Your Classroom | AWW Blog. Retrieved June 1, 2018, from http://blog.awwapp.com/6-cs-of-education-classroom/
5. Whitaker, T., Zoul, J., and Casas, J. (2015). *What Connected Educators Do Differently*. New York: Routledge.
6. Zoul, J. (2017, October 12). Teaching Should Be More Like Coaching. Retrieved June 1, 2018, from http://jeffreyzoul.blogspot.com/2017/10/teaching-should-be-more-like-coaching.html
7. Albert Einstein (n.d.). Retrieved June 1, 2018, from https://en.wikiquote.org/wiki/Albert_Einstein

8. City, E. A., Elmore, R. F., Fiarman, S. E., and Teitel, L. (2014). *Instructional Rounds in Education: A Network Approach to Improving Teaching and Learning*. Cambridge, MA: Harvard Education Press.

9. Mazza, J. and Zoul, J. (2018). *Education Write Now*. New York: Routledge.

10. TED Talks. (2017, May 1). Retrieved June 1, 2018, from www.ted.com/about/programs-initiatives/ted-talks

11. DuFour, R. and Eaker, R. E. (2009). *Professional Learning Communities at Work: Best Practices for Enhancing Student Achievement*. Moorabbin, Vic.: Hawker Brownlow Education.

12. Tech, E. and Office of Ed Tech. (2017, January 18). What Is Personalized Learning? – Personalizing the Learning Experience: Insights from Future Ready Schools – Medium. Retrieved June 1, 2018, from https://medium.com/personalizing-the-learning-experience-insights/what-is-personalized-learning-bc874799b6f

2

Innovative Ways to Impact School Culture

Todd Whitaker

School culture has an incredibly powerful influence on everything we do. Determining ways to continually move it in a positive direction is essential. Our aim is to provide ideas and methods to influence culture in an efficient and effective way.

How come schools are so different from each other? I am not talking about comparing a large urban high school with a small rural elementary. Instead: How come two schools in the same district with similar clientele can seem and feel completely different from each other? This is true whether they are private, public, charter, etc. There is something inherently dissimilar from building to building. What is it? Can we control or even influence it?

In one school it feels that everyone is welcome, friendly, and wants to be there. In a neighboring school, trying to get eye contact from someone when you walk in is difficult and it may feel closer to a glare than a smile. Are they really that different? Can't the people who work there tell? Why doesn't anyone do anything about it? Can they? Is it possible?

What Is This "Culture Thing" Anyhow?

Culture is such a trendy issue. Everything seemingly is about culture. Sports teams have a "culture of winning" or else they want to "change their culture" to become a culture of winning. Companies talk about their "culture of service" or "culture of success," or a "cultural fit." They can be "flat," "open," and "creative," or even "old school synergistic." So many slogans include or describe organizational cultures.

We read about businesses that have ping-pong tables, nap rooms, and total flex schedules. Is this what culture is? Are each of our schools one game/nap room away from teachers having a great culture? Because we claim to have a winning culture or a catchy motto, does that mean we actually do?

Have you ever wondered how often those ping-pong tables are used? Or curious how frequently that nap room is occupied? We all know there can be a difference in how people act when there are visitors, and how a spokesperson can seemingly describe an organization that the people in it do not recognize. We all run the vacuum cleaner just before we have company, and in most families we all know how to put on our "public face" whenever we interact with outsiders. But culture is actually what happens when no one is looking. It's how we relate and communicate – or don't – on a daily basis when there is no special occasion.

> Culture is actually what happens when no one is looking. It's how we relate and communicate – or don't – on a daily basis when there is no special occasion.

Let's take a look at a couple of definitions of culture. Hofstede describes culture as a "collective programming of the mind which distinguishes the members of one organization from another" (1997, p.180). Programming of the mind is an intriguing concept, isn't it? Schein has a more basic description stating that culture is a social indoctrination of unwritten rules that people learn as they try to fit in to a particular group (1992). We all want to fit in, don't we? – at least some of the time?

If culture provides the guidelines for how to fit in to our organization or school then it is a pretty powerful force that makes it tough to resist. And what about the nugget in Schein's definition that the rules are "unwritten?" How do we learn these things? Is this a positive or a negative? To some degree it may even sound like Orwell's book *1984*. To some degree maybe it is.

We may think of culture as a superpower. And we have all seen enough superhero movies to know that some characters use these extra skills for good and others may, at least at times, focus on evil. Don't worry. This is not an attempt to scare you. And since we are fortunate to be in the field of education, the vast majority of people are in it for the right reasons: To have a positive impact on students, to make a difference, etc. Though this is also true with the people in a struggling school, something is keeping these efforts from coming to fruition. What is it that is keeping them from having the type of collective educational setting that they all individually hope for?

Let's make a quick comparison between climate and culture. According to Gruenert and Whitaker (2015), Figure 2.1 shows some of the ways they can be compared.

Obviously it is much easier to change an attitude than a personality. We can go from a good mood to a bad one or vice versa quite readily and frequently. In many schools there is a vastly different tone on Monday versus Friday. You can just imagine the change in mood when an announcement is made that school is cancelled tomorrow due to weather. These are pretty intuitive. However, let's look at a couple of the next items from the list in Figure 2.1.

Culture	Climate
The group's personality	The group's attitude
Gives permission to be miserable on Mondays	Differs from Monday to Friday, February to May
Provides for a limited way of thinking	Creates a state of mind
Can't be felt, even by group members	Can be felt when you enter a room
Is the way we do things around here	Is the way we feel around here
Determines whether or not improvement is possible	Is the first thing that improves when positive change is made
Is in your head	Is in your head

FIGURE 2.1
Source: Gruenert and Whitaker (2015, p.10)

Culture provides for a limited way of thinking. Sounds almost cult like, doesn't it? Well, it sort of is. Now realize, it is like those superpowers – it can be a positive or a negative. If the culture is a positive one in nature, it may limit the amount of complaining that does not lead to a solution. Inversely if it is a more negative tone, it may allow and even encourage fault finding and negativity so that it pulls everyone down even if their mood (climate) did not start at this point.

What is really interesting is that people within an organization may be less able to identify the culture than outsiders. What happens, especially over time, is that the environment we find ourselves in can eventually, and at times quickly, become normalized. The teachers' lounge can become a place where we put our gripe on. Department or grade-level meetings may come up with more problems than solutions. We start to think of this as normal. The opposite can also be true. We can feel frustrated in our classroom but uplifted when we get with our colleagues in the faculty lunchroom. We have trouble solving a teaching challenge and our department meeting is the ideal place to find potential options. Either way, this becomes what we expect and we tend to the think this is what the world is like.

However, if we leave and go into a new setting we may find a completely different scenario. The person who is new to an organization often has – for a limited time – the most ability to actually identify what the culture is, because after a while it becomes normal to them also. It is sort of like a marriage. We may have had a vision prior to nuptials but over time we assimilate our vision or a marriage to what our everyday relationship is. This may be a positive or a negative, but it eventually becomes a part of ourselves.

The final two points of the list may be most revealing when it comes to the power of culture. The culture can determine whether or not improvement is possible. Have you ever been in an organization where it seems that one of two people determine the fate of an idea? If Don Downer doesn't like it, is it quickly discarded? Or do we need to wait and see what the grade 2 team thinks before it is a yay or a nay? Maybe there has even been a culture where things like, "We have always done it this way" or "It won't work with our students" become the controlling mantra.

These are examples where a seemingly mysterious power – i.e., the culture – takes over.

The last, and maybe most significant point, is that both culture and climate exist in our heads. There really is no concrete measure. It is how each person views the school. Think of it as the difference between a growth mindset and a fixed mindset: One stops you from looking for solutions and the other expects you to find one. Culture can be like a blanket or cloud over the school to determine whether we look to solve a puzzle or instead turn to hopelessness as an excuse. So potentially, to change a culture we must have to change the minds of people in the organization. Let's get started.

3–5–7 Years?

Many people who focus on school culture talk about how long it takes to change one, and the majority of experts say 3 to 5 to 7 years. Let's see if we can speed that process up. We actually *have to* accelerate it. The reason is simple: What we do is so important that we cannot wait that long to improve a school. If you have school-age children you have little interest in that school improving in 3 to 7 years, because then your child will no longer be a student there. Your desires have now moved on to a new setting.

> Improving culture is a continuous process rather than an event. We don't make a step forward, exhale and exclaim that we are glad that is over with. Instead it is a continual effort and it needs to be intentional.

We also have to understand that improving culture is a continuous process rather than an event. We don't make a step forward, exhale, and exclaim that we are glad that is over with. Instead it is a continual effort and it needs to be intentional to have the desired result.

No Magic Bean

No one likes to be the bearer of bad news, but there is no magic bean when it comes to improving culture. It doesn't happen by accident and there are no shortcuts. However, there are ways to expedite and improve the process. It involves work and not trite sayings.

Telling people to innovate, innovate, innovate does nothing to move a culture forward. Instead it actually makes the status quo culture stronger and more resistant. When a culture thinks it is threatened by someone wanting to change it, the culture and its members circle the wagons to resist the threat. If you want to improve or alter a culture, do not let the culture know that you want to change it. You cannot mandate effectiveness. People are inherently contrarians – at least many people are – and they often have a great deal of influence (usually a disproportionate amount) over an organization.

People ask me to do workshops for their groups on a regular basis. Someone will ask me to do a workshop on team building: I say sure and let's call it "team building" so that way everyone can vomit at the same time. Instead, let's just do a workshop without any reference to team building and have components of it be *interactive*. That way there is not an inherent resistance to the concept. When the workshop is completed and attendees found it of value, they will be much more receptive to the parts where we all interacted rather than being resistant to a direct attack on the culture by implying they need more team building.

You Start Undefeated

There is a reason businesses rebrand. There is a reason education and schools seemingly recycle programs under new names. The previous rendition has too much baggage and needs a fresh start. That is also the reason why the first faculty meeting of the year is so essential to altering a culture: Because the culture is less established then. There is optimism and hope that this year will be different – be better. Additionally there are new faculty and staff that do not have a sense of what the culture is. Since it exists in our minds, new staff members are often a place to start when moving a culture forward. Typically the culture likes to look backwards – that way it stays in place. However, to alter the culture we must look forward so that people see a different vision in their minds. The start of a new year is the perfect place to begin that process.

Think of it this way. Where is the enthusiasm level of a new teacher? At the start of the year it is sky high. The first goal is to keep it there. Even the least enthusiastic of the veteran teachers usually have a more positive disposition at the beginning of the year. We must work to keep it there if possible. Doing so is much easier than raising it once the tone drops.

Leadership

Leadership and culture can at times be used almost interchange-ably. A school that has a positive culture usually has a positive leader. If a school has a poor culture then they typically have a poor leader.

Though we might think of a culture "outlasting" the leader there may actually be more connection than we may intuitively think. People talk about a "winning culture" of sports teams. We often hear of it when we think of college football and basketball teams. Alabama, Michigan, and Ohio State have winning cultures when it comes to football and Kentucky, Duke, and North Carolina come to mind when we think of winning cultures in basketball programs. If we are going to give all of the credit to the culture, how come each of these programs have had ups and downs? Since it is the culture, why would a new leader impact it so greatly?

In the last decade Alabama has been the cream of the crop in college football. Yet before Nick Saban went there they were in a down cycle. How come? Could it be the leader? Well, you can probably answer that question yourself. If Nick Saban left Alabama and swapped positions with an unsuccessful coach at another school do you think that unsuccessful coach would be multi-time national champions at Alabama and Coach Saban would struggle through multiple losing seasons at his new locale? How long would it take to see any change?

Does North Carolina have a winning basketball culture or have Dean Smith and Roy Williams been successful leaders?

Remember there was a coach in between them who struggled mightily with the same culture – and he was even a former player who knew the culture inside and out. How is that possible? Maybe it is leadership or lack thereof.

We can see how important leadership is at the top of the food chain – i.e., the head coach, principal, or superintendent, but we must also understand how important it is at all levels in an organization. One of the biggest challenges a coach faces is that often their best player is not their best leader. Since they are the "best player" they often set the example for the rest of the team rather than the person who the coach most hopes others will emulate. This is exactly what happens in many school settings.

One of the trendy things to say is the famous quote by David Weinberger, "The smartest person in the room, is the room." On one level it is true. Or at least we *wish* it were true. If we could draw from all of the knowledge of a group of people we would make a better decision than if we used the knowledge of only one person to make a decision. Our instinct may be that this "group think" is still better than traditional top–down thinking which is when, in a school, the principal makes decisions without the input of others. We can easily see the limits of taking this approach: The people "in the trenches" are left out and may have the most knowledge of what would work best in practice. As a result another chant has now become common when looking to make the best decisions in a school. That is "Collaboration, collaboration, collaboration." Again, in an ideal world where we actually do make decisions based on the smartest person and the collective wisdom, there is no better method. However, many places do not operate in this fashion.

In some school settings a teacher who is a former athlete may have way more influence than knowledge. A person who is wealthier, married to someone "important," or more attractive may carry much more sway than skill. This is why it is so essential to connect leadership with influence and ability. If at all possible we want to make sure the ability to lead aligns with the most talented person. This way the smartest person in the room is actually the room.

Not only should this be done on a school-wide basis, it is essential that it follows a similar pattern at all levels. Let's take a look at subcultures and how important they are to a school's success.

Subcultures

Though the overall culture ultimately determines the direction of an organization, subcultures can have a significant impact on smaller areas of a school. Typically everyone who is part of a culture also aligns with several subcultures in that building. We can connect with our grade 3 colleagues, be part of a group of coaches, interact with other teachers who are new parents, and have a common lunch with six others who belong to none of the above groups. Each of these subcultures can pull and tug us in varying directions. Maybe the coaches look for ways to zip out of the building as soon as the day ends. Our grade 3 colleagues may have instructional pressures that no one else faces because this grade is under the microscope due to the standardized testing in our state. New parents have their own dynamic, and the lunch group could have a totally different feel. Additionally, the way we interact in each may vary and we may be someone who cross-pollinates the group by carrying messages from one to the other.

Often the changing nature of our interactions and the mood from one group to the next is due to the subculture. There is a different *expectation* about how we act with each group. It's a little like when a teenager is with their parents, friends, or boy/girl-friend. They may have three different "personas" they display as needed. The stress may be when these subgroups cross paths.

Changing a culture often needs to start from a subculture. If the grade 3 teachers are doing something more effective or original than another grade level, the teacher who connects with other subgroups can be a salesperson for this new idea. However, if they do not establish connectivity with the other clusters, then the influence is minimal. And these interactions run both ways. Imagine if a grade 3 teacher, who was also a member of the new parents' subculture group, learned at the new parent group about a more effective approach: This teacher could then share with grade 3 colleagues during their subculture time.

Remember subcultures are just like cultures. There is no good or bad that is automatically affiliated with any of them. Positivity and negativity can both be shared in this same manner. It is important that an organization works to make sure the right people are the influencers so that the smartest person in the room can actually be the room.

> It is important that an organization works to make sure the right people are the influencers so that the smartest person in the room can actually be the room.

Collaboration can also have a negative effect. If the strongest and most influential personalities are not positive and productive then their opinion may carry much more weight than it should. In this setting, the more we collaborate the more we may actually restrict innovation. We must be aware that most aspects of a culture – such as collaboration, influence, and subcultures – are vehicles more than they are directional. They determine how fast or slow we go. They do not necessarily ensure we move in a positive direction.

Climate

Though climate and culture are often used interchangeably, they are very different beasts. Each is significant and, although they may overlap and are connected, they can vary greatly.

A married couple can be having a dispute at a store but they can fake smiles when they happen on someone from their church for a few minutes. They can give an all-is-well veneer. This is climate. The dispute may be temporary and clearly the switch to grins is also. This is how come so many cultural alterations have to start as a climate change.

If we want to greet all students in a warm and welcoming fashion we need someone in the school to do it one time. Now that is climate for that teacher and that class that day. However, if that teacher does it every day it becomes a "classroom culture" for his or her students. If the other teachers in the hallway take the same approach then this becomes a hallway subculture. By this being a subculture it becomes expected for each teacher in that hallway to greet the students with a smile even when they don't feel like it. If another teacher comes into that hallway they will get a sense or even be told the expectation that in this hallway we all greet the students.

Now when one of those teachers switches classrooms and is in a different hallway, at some point it will be determined if they have the resolve to continue when they are the only one to offer greetings in the new location. If they do, and they have the influence to get others on board in the new locale, then they can help spread the "virus." If they stop because it is not the "norm" in the new hallway, then the culture "wins" and they have become like the culture.

This may seem like a simplistic example but this is how individuals, subcultures, and cultures interconnect. If an individual has enough strength and influence they can start and spread a new pattern of behavior. If this individual can connect with new staff members who do not know the "unwritten rules" of the school they can make this happen even more quickly. One of the roles of a leader is to increase the likelihood of this happening. By making sure the new teachers get assigned to mentors who are exhibiting a target value, it can help spread the culture more quickly. Thinking of room location, plan times, lunch times, etc., can help connect new staff members with individuals or subcultures that need to be expanded.

Conversely there may be less positive people – or even those who long for the good old days (rearview mirror) who want to guard the culture and work to have the new staff members join their coffee crew (subculture). Keep in mind that every school has multiple welcoming committees – formal and informal – for new staff members. We must ensure that they get membership into the right ones.

> Keep in mind that every school has multiple welcoming committees – formal and informal – for new staff members. We must ensure that they get membership into the right ones.

The connections between subcultures and climate can be significant, and they are both the entry points to altering culture.

Think of it this way. If today we greet all students in the school, we change the climate (not the culture since it is just one day). However, if every day we greet the students, eventually we change the culture. When this shift from climate to culture actually occurs is up to debate. Whether it moves from climate to culture is not. There are times we have to change behaviors (climate) before we can change beliefs (culture).

If the current culture in a school is not one where all students are greeted by everyone in a warm and welcoming manner, every day the culture actually works toward preventing that from happening. Co-workers may even ask the breakthrough positive person why they are so happy today in a challenging way to help them learn what is "normal" in this school. However, if at some point the culture in a school is one where all students are greeted in a warm and welcoming manner each day, the culture will work toward keeping that in place. The teacher who is not smiling may be asked what is wrong and at some point greeted with derision since they are swaying from the positive culture that exists. This same example applies in each of the subcultures in both directions.

Expanding Positive Influences

This chapter is titled "Innovative Ways to Impact School Culture." You might be thinking what is so innovative about these ideas? Well, nothing actually. Yet everything. The reason that they are innovative is that very few people attempt, or especially have success in, altering a culture. The reason the ideas are not so innovative is that these exact same ideas have worked since it was decided organizations should have a positive culture.

If a person joins the science department in a high school, the subculture of that department will work to get them to join the fold. When the department goes to the first school assembly the new teacher will often ask other science teachers what they are supposed to do at assemblies. If their co-workers say, "we just drop them off and come back to our rooms" that likely will become the new norm for that teacher. If the peer says, "we sit with our students and especially try to sit next to the students who are most likely to converse" then that is likely to become the new norm. For this reason, we work to have new staff members connect with positive peers.

But what if they are joining a grade level, team, or department that does not have the subculture we would hope? If you would like to be happy and perky at work every day but your grade-level colleagues are not of the same mindset, you had better find some others who would like to be happy and perky every day. If you do not, you might find yourself becoming miserable like them. But what if you are in a small school and you are the only grade 3 teacher, the only band teacher, or the only physics teacher. Now what? Obviously you can seek out others who are at different grades or subjects, but the culture may not encourage that connectivity. Another choice is to use social media to find these "empowerers" (Whitaker et al., 2016). By connecting with others anywhere, we can establish a subculture that will enable us to be a stronger staff member while we are looking for those within our school to bond with. Additionally, we can garner ideas from those outside our school, which may expand our knowledge base to enable us to more effectively influence others within our setting.

Another important way to align influence and ability within a school is to have teachers observe their colleagues. Not only is this a powerful learning and growing opportunity, but it also allows the influence of more effective staff members to expand while simultaneously diminishing the power of less effective teachers. This is not an effort to deride anyone – quite the opposite. It allows the knowledge of one teacher to become the knowledge of all teachers. No one steals a poor idea. So if staff members have the opportunity to observe and learn from others it really does help all teachers to become like the best teachers.

Another positive benefit of observing colleagues is that it helps everyone become aware of who *should* be the most influential staff members in the school. And it really can have a quick impact by aligning ability and informal power within subcultures at grade levels and departments. If I am a new staff member and I have not observed other teachers I might be swayed by who is the most outgoing or who has the strongest personality. Some teachers are also better at self-promoting than others. This is not necessarily bad, but it does not mean these teachers teach as well as they talk. By having the chance to actually observe colleagues, we have more ability to see who can actually help us in our own classrooms. It can also help us determine whom we most want to align with. If our heart is set on having the greatest positive impact possible with students, we desperately want to find other teachers who have the same focus and desire.

Visiting classrooms in a non-judgmental, non-evaluative manner is an opportunity to observe and learn from others in our location. Social media is clearly a way to do this with people in all locations. Then we can see how to do things in our own setting with our clientele and our resources. Even if there are many teachers who would resist this and possibly refuse, we are still better off if some teachers learn from others, than not at all. Oftentimes the people who first choose to participate are the best teachers and the new teachers. There is no more powerful sub-culture to impact the overall culture than when these two groups align – and the more the merrier. As more teachers participate in this valuable learning experience, the subculture becomes more significant and eventually may actually become the overall culture of the school.

Conclusion

The introduction to this chapter started with these sentences: "School culture has an incredibly powerful influence on everything we do. Determining ways to continually move it in a positive direction is essential." These are truths. What we do with them is up to us.

Though we may feel that culture is an immovable object with insurmountable odds, it actually is a living and breathing organism in every school. Each interaction we have determines the direction it is going. We can disagree with how long it takes to change a school culture; but we can all agree that the best time to start is now.

References

Gruenert, S. and Whitaker, T. (2015). *School Culture Rewired: How to Define, Assess and Transform It*. Alexandria, VA: ASCD.

Hofstede, G. (1997). *Culture and Organizations: Software for the Mind*. New York: McGraw-Hill.

Schein, E. (1992). *Organizational Culture and Leadership*, 2nd ed. San Francisco, CA: Jossey-Bass.

Whitaker, T., Whitaker, M., and Whitaker, K. (2016). *Your First Year: How to Survive and Thrive as a New Teacher*. New York: Routledge.

3

Innovating Our Hiring Practices

Jimmy Casas

There are only two ways to improve schools. Hire better teachers or improve the ones you already have. – Todd Whitaker

Leading a school can be a messy endeavor, even for the most experienced and skilled leaders. What we expect in terms of teacher performance, how we motivate staff to excel at high levels, and more importantly, how we model excellence ourselves, can all make a difference. This is especially true if we aspire to expand our sphere of influence in order to create the conditions for success for both our staff and our schools.

For some schools, with each new year comes countless numbers of retirements, resignations, and in some cases, budget cuts. For other schools, they may be experiencing growth in enrollment, resulting in the opportunity for new personnel. Regardless of the reasons for new additions in staff, what we know is that ultimately these changes impact staffing plans in school districts across the country, creating new opportunities for us to bring in a new wave of personnel to positively, or, if we are not careful, negatively, impact our school cultures.

Yet what should be seen by school leaders as a golden opportunity is often viewed by many as burdensome. Bringing new staff into our organizations, especially during the closing months of a school year, can lead to increases in stress levels for school administrators, even more so when turnover is high. Each new hire comes with a myriad of steps that need to take place in order to ensure that we are bringing in new people who are deemed as excellent; each step requiring more and more time, thus, causing us sometimes to rush through the process. Ironically, even though most school and district leaders would argue that there is nothing more important than hiring the best teachers in order to significantly increase the chances for student success, we sometimes forget this very notion due to a plethora of other tasks needing action coming at us on a daily basis. In doing so, we forget this simple, but most important basic thought:

> *The most important responsibility we have as school leaders is to hire the best people, yet it remains the area in which we invest the least amount of time in terms of importance.*

If the above statement is an accurate portrayal of your current state, then we must begin to ask ourselves: Why did we fall back to a practice that is mediocre at best, especially knowing the lasting impact this has on students and their achievement levels? If you are still reading this chapter, then maybe it is because you no longer want to be satisfied with the status quo and you are ready to move forward with a new approach to bringing in new people into your organization.

Almost ten years ago, the administrative team with whom I worked made the intentional decision to begin to think differently about how we as a team approached the hiring process, ultimately leading us to revamp our practices knowing that we had to begin to think and act differently if we were going to move our school culture to a higher level of excellence. This new approach would require us to change our mindset and more importantly, our behavior. This new process, led and modeled by the principal, would encompass the following practices:

- ◆ Focus more on relationships and personalizing the experience for each candidate.
- ◆ Model the behaviors that would support our core beliefs and inspire others to do the same.
- ◆ Set a standard of high expectations that expected excellence from ourselves and the candidates.

The premise behind this process was to have each candidate who applied and was contacted and/or interviewed say, "I wish I could work for that administrative team" and/or "I want to work in that school." That was our mindset and we were going to do everything we could during the hiring process to leave such a lasting impression and more importantly, an experience like no other, that would inspire the best candidates to want to be a part of our school and propel us to the next level of excellence. The steps described below served as a framework for our practices that we followed with each new hire.

Emphasize the Initial Contact

If principals are going to say that relationships are the foundation of all of our work and that we believe there is not a more important factor in determining the success of our students and staff, then we must begin the initial process by not just talking about the importance of relationships, but actually modeling it in making the initial contact.

In an era of advanced technology and trying to save time, many schools have moved toward integrating technology to generate electronic communications to potential candidates, including email confirmations of applications being completed or received, reference checks, interview schedules, and post-interview communications. This practice goes against the fundamental principle of fostering personal relationships, thus sending mixed messages to candidates. When the principal or a member of his/her administrative team calls a candidate, it provides an opportunity for the candidate to sense your passion, to feel your enthusiasm, and to connect with you. When the principal makes the initial call to a candidate, it sends a strong message to the candidate that the principal is passionate about her/his work and that she/he is willing to do the front-line work that is sometimes absent in our own work.

> When the principal makes the initial call to a candidate, it sends a strong message to the candidate that the principal is passionate about her/his work and that she/he is willing to do the front-line work.

Be Flexible

It is important that we make sure that we are flexible during the hiring process, especially when it comes to scheduling interviews. Rather than tie candidates into a specific day or timeslot, consider giving them more choices from which to select. If candidates express to you that the timeslots you have offered for them don't work, then work together with the candidate to find a date and time that does work. The practice of being rigid and not providing alternative options reflects poorly on us and screams, "It's more about us than it is about you the candidate." In a previous school where I have worked, if the candidate was not able to make the scheduled time that we had provided, we simply moved on to the next candidate. Looking back on those experiences, I now believe we responded poorly.

> *Let's aim to be flexible and send the message that this is not about us (the school); rather it is about them (the candidate).*

Put Candidates at Ease

Once the interview is scheduled we should provide as much information as possible to help put the candidate at ease. This could/should include who will be involved in the interview process, the length of the interview, what the interview will entail, how many questions will be asked, what to prepare, where to park, and where to enter the building, etc.

> *Be intentional in your approach by providing the information necessary in order to put the candidate at ease and allow them to demonstrate their best.*

Set Them Up for Success

Before the interview begins, let the candidate know the first question in order to put them at ease. Sample questions could include, "Tell us about yourself: What led you to apply for this position?" or "What do you enjoy most about teaching and how do you keep the fire burning inside year after year?" We should take time to try and extrapolate from the candidate their passion, why they do what they do, who or what inspired them, and what have they enjoyed most in their journey, as well as hear about the challenges they continue to face. By doing so this allows us to get to know the candidate on a more personal level.

Get to know the candidate as a person, to listen to his/her story, in order to take another step in building a relationship with him/her.

Teach a Lesson

One expectation for candidates is to have them demonstrate their ability to connect with students by requiring them to teach a lesson. Length of time can vary, but I would recommend anywhere between 30 and 45 minutes. Connect the candidate with the classroom teacher to share information about the class, including the current content and topics being taught, details about past and current student struggles and successes, and all other pertinent information including class size, room arrangement, available technology, etc. Focus should be not only on delivery of instruction but just as important, a focus on ability to connect with students in a genuine manner that leaves the students wanting the teacher to come back. It is important that we maintain the same level of high standards for our candidates as we have of ourselves in establishing a climate whereby students feel welcomed and valued. This demonstrates to all candidates that you want them to be successful and that student voice is something to take very seriously, especially when it comes to connecting with students. This will help you determine if they have a "Students 1st" mindset.

Student voice is something to take very seriously, especially when it comes to connecting with students. This will help you determine if they have a "Students 1st" mindset.

Carefully Select the Interview Team

Too often we don't take enough time to think about who should be on the interview team, instead falling back to what we have always done. For example, hiring a math teacher? Let's include all of the math teachers on the interview team. Replacing a grade 4 teacher? Guess we should allow the entire grade 4 team to be on the team, right? Not necessarily. Perhaps we need to be more strategic and spend more time thinking through who we want on the team that would make more sense than just falling in line with what we have always done. One thought would be to select a team of teachers that you believe are your best teachers. After all, why wouldn't we want our best people to assist us in in identifying those attributes of excellence that the best teachers possess? Or perhaps it would be a good idea to include a varied group of people with different skill sets to help us identify what our school team is lacking that a new candidate might be able to provide. Not to be forgotten, would it not behoove us to identify which staff members would be working closely with this person, thus cultivating a stronger sense of team, beginning with the hiring process? For example, perhaps when replacing that grade 4 teacher, rather than include all grade 4 teachers, it may be more beneficial to include a grade 3 teacher and a grade 5 teacher to help us create a more aligned and cohesive team. We might also want to consider including a counselor, instructional coach, or even a special education teacher to round out the team.

> *Foster a closer community of teachers by choosing a different group of invested teachers for the interview team, rather than continuing with past practices that take the easy path.*

Clarify the Role of the Committee

Ever wonder why some staff feel jilted after serving on an interview team? My experience in this process has led me to believe that it's because we as an administrative team did not do a very good job of clarifying and communicating the roles and responsibilities of the interview team. By neglecting to be clear up front, we unintentionally gave the impression to the hiring team that they were going to decide who the next hire was going to be. Let me state that the most important role of a building principal is to hire the staff. This function should never be relinquished to a group of teachers or a committee. Do we want and need staff involved in the hiring of new staff? Of course. But their role should be limited to providing feedback that will help the principal determine his/her next round of new hires. Think about it this way. First, teachers were never trained on how to hire personnel, so why would we put that responsibility on them when they don't have that experience? Second, I don't believe teachers evaluate, promote, monitor progress, or fire teachers. Principals do. So if the principal is going to carry this heavy load, then wouldn't we expect them to make the final decision on whom to bring on board?

When preparing to form an advisory committee to help you with insight and feedback on potential candidates, principals must communicate up front and clearly that the role of the committee is not to hire the next candidate, but to share their thoughts, reflections, and opinions on the strengths, talents, and shortcomings of the candidate based solely on their interactions with the candidate during the interview process. When we follow a well-defined process and communicate clearly up front the roles and expectations of those staff who are part of the process, then we end up with better results. If we plan on utilizing staff in the hiring process (and I feel strongly that we should), then we must do a better job of coaching our people on a process that can be clearly communicated, understood, and agreed upon by all members in a positive way before the process ever begins.

The Interview Process

We must establish protocols for the process and then be vigilant in seeing them through. One common mistake made when interviewing more than one candidate is to not set forth a protocol for discussing candidates in a fair manner. More often than not we allow committee members to discuss candidates after each interview in an informal manner, often allowing committee members to be influenced (both positively and negatively) by other members of the committee. This can be problematic in instances when members are highly regarded as leaders, or in worse cases, regarded as intimidating and having a negative influence over others. We must guarantee a fair process where all candidates are discussed in a fair and transparent manner with all members present and engaged.

> We must guarantee a fair process where all candidates are discussed in a fair and transparent manner with all members present and engaged.

Don't Allow Ranking of Candidates

When all candidates have been interviewed and discussions have taken place with everyone present, and everyone has been given the opportunity to express their thoughts, opinions, and provide honest feedback on each candidate, then ranking of candidates should *never* be allowed. If allowed, this can create a division among committee members.

Consider a scenario in which Candidate A is ranked by some members on the committee as their first choice, and ranked second by the rest of the members except one who ranked that candidate as their third choice. Now imagine that this candidate is eventually selected via a ranking system, so that the administrative team has now created a division amongst the committee. In this scenario, the committee member who ranked the candidate third is going to walk away extremely disappointed due to the fact that we just selected a candidate who was their third choice. Even those who ranked the candidate as their second choice may leave with a bitter taste in their mouths.

By following a process where candidates are ranked in order we begin to create a divisive culture based on winners and losers. A much better process would be to include on the common scoring rubric a question that asks the following; "Could you work with this person? Why or why not?" or "Is this person a good fit for our/your team?" This allows for more discussion where members share their reasons for why they could(n't) work with this team. Oftentimes, committee members will have more than one candidate they feel is a good fit or they could work with as part of their team. Regardless of who the principal ultimately selects, the committee will be more likely to walk away satisfied, knowing they were fine with either candidate being selected.

Always avoid processes that potentially leave participants feeling dissatisfied with the end result.

Conduct Better Reference Checks

Many districts currently use a standard set of questions when calling for reference checks. Questions may include the typical inquiries on a candidate's attendance, overall performance, judgment, strengths, areas of improvement, etc. However, the most commonly asked question when conducting reference checks includes a question along these lines, "Is this person eligible for rehire?" or "If given the opportunity, would you rehire this person?" I am not convinced from my experience that either one of these is the right question we want to ask. I understand why we ask it, but I think there is a better way to phrase the question that will help us determine whether or not we want to bring this person on board. When asked in this manner it leaves the potential for a "yes" answer not because the person wants to hire them back, but rather because they have to hire them back because they have no other options. This happens in those districts where pools are limited or qualified candidates are a scarcity. These scenarios leave a district answering "yes" to these two questions not because they are excited about the prospect of bringing the employee back, but rather because they are limited in their options.

A better question might sound something like: "If you were to take a new position in a different district, would you actively recruit this person to come work for you in your new school because you felt strongly you had to have them on your staff?"

A response to this question would tell me a lot more about their level of confidence and desire to want to continue having this person on their team.

In addition, I would use the following recruitment strategy when calling for a reference check. Let's presume we are hiring a grade 7 social studies teacher. I would ask: "How many social studies teachers do you have in your school?" Once a response had been given, I would follow up by asking them to rank the candidate in relation to the other social studies teachers in their building. The ideal scenario here is that they would answer with a definitive ranking of number one. After all, who wants someone's fourth best social studies teacher? We want their best teacher, so hopefully the response to our question would be a resounding number one!

The best reference checks are the ones where the person doing the reference check is diving deeper into the questions by asking more follow-up questions. Always be wary of general responses such as he/she is "wonderful," "great," "parents love him/her," and "kids are sad to see him/her leave." We have a responsibility to ask the right questions during the reference checks.

Be prepared to follow up with "Why?" And another "Why?" to that response. And ask for an example. And maybe even a final "Why?"

Follow Up with All Candidates

I believe strongly that all candidates who interview for a position should be given the courtesy of a phone call regardless of whether they are offered a position. If you yourself or a loved one has ever interviewed for a position where there was never a follow-up call, well, you know exactly how that feels, so why would we ever want one of our candidates to be left with that same empty feeling? We should never allow that to happen. Simply put, all candidates deserve to get a call.

We have a responsibility to our profession to help those who were not selected and to provide them with honest feedback about why they were not selected. That is the least we can do. If you believe a candidate has the necessary skills to be successful in the classroom but fell short in the quest for a position in your building for whatever reason, then I think we need to go a step further and help that person with a follow-up conversation detailing what they can do in your opinion to increase their likelihood of finding a position the next time around.

In some cases, I think we can go even further by reaching out to our colleagues and putting in a good word. When a future educator has the skills and potential to be a great educator someday, we need to do everything possible to support him/her and in turn, support our profession. We need great teachers in our classrooms, no matter where that classroom may be.

> When a future educator has the skills and potential to be a great educator someday, we need to do everything possible to support him/her and in turn, support our profession.

Be Intentional with Making the Offer

There is something special about preparing to call a candidate to whom you intend to offer a position. For obvious reasons, this call is much easier to make than the call to tell someone that they didn't get the job. When making this call it is important to take into consideration that during most hiring processes, if we have invested ample time, we have learned quite a bit about the candidate. However, often left out is the fact that our processes don't leave much opportunity for the candidates to get to know us. Hence, why this last step is so critical and should not be overlooked when making an offer. We must be intentional in these final moments to invite the candidate back in (when reasonable, and if not, then a follow-up conference call) before offering a position. By providing this opportunity, you give yourself permission to spend time with the candidate, allowing them to get to know you on a more personal basis.

Conclusion

As I reflect back on the opening quote in this chapter by Todd Whitaker, it pushes me to question, "Could there be a third way to improve schools?" Perhaps a third solution lies in our approach to how we hire new staff. When we are genuinely intentional in our approach and focus on the fundamental belief that there is nothing more important than building relationships, then we have a duty, better yet, an *obligation* to model the very core behavior that we believe is the driving force in any culture of excellence – relationships. When we are committed to investing in each candidate in order to provide a meaningful experience where the principal shares his/her core values in order for the candidate to get to truly understand his/her vision and expectations, we end up with a candidate who better understands us and ultimately, is even more excited about working for us. And if they should not be so fortunate to get selected for the position, the way we behave lends itself for them to look back and say, "I wanted that job so badly!" The more deposits that we make throughout the hiring process, the more likelihood of a positive return on our investment and a win for our school community.

4

Innovative Learning Spaces

Thomas C. Murray

Expecting today's modern learners to maximize their potential and develop the needed skills for tomorrow's workforce, in a one-size-fits-all, sit-and-get, teacher-centric environment is simply educational malpractice. With all that we know about how students learn, all of the socially connected resources we have at our fingertips, and all of the innovative ways in which learning experiences are transforming in schools around the country, not evolving our practices to align with the needs of our students is a disservice to what today's learners both need and deserve.

Over the past few years, the notion of "learning-space redesign" has become a trendy phrase and popular focus in educational circles. Search virtually any social media platform and images of fancy classroom designs, "flexible seating," and Starbucks comparisons are plentiful. Some schools find themselves investing tens of thousands of dollars in new furniture, while for most schools, financing for tangible things such as expensive chairs and tables is not, and may never be, feasible. Yet, educators are undoubtedly some of the most creative, thoughtful, dynamic innovators on the planet. Those with very limited budgets, complemented with an intentional vision of student learning, are finding ways to mindfully design the spaces today's learners need.

Designing innovative learning spaces does not start with writing checks to places that sell trendy furniture. It starts with the mindset and awareness of those who have the privilege to serve students each and every day. So how can innovative spaces be designed for today's modern learners?

Be Intentional: Start with the Why

When you know your why, your what has more impact, because you are walking in or towards your purpose.
– Michael Jr.

To design innovative learning spaces, we must remain focused on the *purpose* of our intentions. At a time when social media glorifies the latest trend, designing spaces to keep up with the latest Pinterest board can be tempting. But if we're not careful, getting caught in the latest trend can also be a colossal waste of precious resources.

Simon Sinek (2009), well-known author and speaker, highlights how every organization, and every person within it, operates on three levels: *What* we do, *How* we do it, and *Why* we do what we do. Whether it's the product one sells, the latest EdTech company, or the local elementary school, Sinek lays out his case that everyone knows what they do, some know how they do it, but very few can clearly articulate why they do what they do. It's those that understand and can articulate the WHY, that stand head and shoulders above the rest.

Sinek's "Golden Circle," consisting of three concentric circles that resemble a bullseye, puts WHAT in the outer ring, HOW in the middle ring, and WHY at the center (see Figure 4.1). He shares how the two inner sections of the Golden Circle, the WHY and the HOW, correspond to the middle section of the human brain and the limbic system – the system responsible for all of one's decision making and behavior as well as one's feelings such as trust. Sinek postulates that it's this portion of the brain which often gives one their "gut instinct" and helps people to understand their purpose. Therefore, it's imperative that we tap

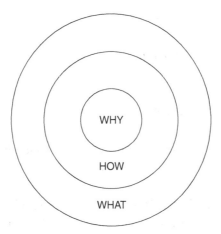

FIGURE 4.1

this portion of the brain in our decision making to redesign the spaces for our learners.

So why should we design learning spaces differently from those that many of us experienced as students ourselves? Why should we spend our precious time and effort on something like design when there are countless other tasks on our plates? In an era of initiative overload in my school, why should learning-space design even be on my radar?

"Us," "our," and "my" as used in the commonly asked questions above show an inherent mindset, and set of priorities, in the questions themselves. In all that we do, it's vital to remember that our work in schools is *not about us*. It's all about them; the students that we serve. So what is it that today's modern learners need?

As we remain focused on the WHY – *our purpose* – it's imperative to understand the need for today's students to have dynamic and authentic learning opportunities, be engaged on high-level tasks, and have spaces to design and create, spaces for play and social interactions, and even spaces for quiet reflection. These are ideas that we'll break down as we start to look at the HOW and the WHAT throughout the rest of this chapter.

Whether it's branding the message of your school, shifting educational paradigms, or redesigning learning spaces, remaining hyperfocused on the WHY of the transformation is paramount to success and long-term sustainability. Change is never easy, but our students are always worth it.

Designing a Learner-Centered Space

Vision is the art of seeing what is invisible to others.
– Jonathan Swift

When I reflect on the early portion of my teaching career, I can remember spending countless hours each summer designing the learning space – for me. Desks were placed neatly in rows, each facing the front board, with a large space up front for me to "do the teaching." Such a design articulated that this classroom was clearly prepared for me to be the "sage on the stage." With quiet force, it screamed that I was there to disseminate information and that I would be transferring the information to students as they sat, islands unto themselves. At that point in my career, I was completely unaware of the profound impact design has on the way students learn. Yet decades later, growth in learning sciences and my own understanding has been significant.

If students had entered my classroom prior to the first day of school, and observed the space on their own, what would they have internalized about my teaching and learning philosophies? How would they interpret such "design language?" Would it have appeared that the space was more about me or more about them? What would they have thought about my own beliefs about teaching and learning, by simply taking in the space? As I reflect on that time, I suspect that they would have believed that the space indicated that I was there to provide them content, and they were there to absorb it.

To understand how to design learner-centered spaces, we need to understand what evidence reveals to have the most impact on the brain. Focusing on the why, and understanding how the brain works, will help us design the innovative spaces that today's modern learners need to thrive. Cognitive psychologists, often referred to as "brain scientists" explore the mental processes of people by studying how the brain works; how one thinks, remembers, and ultimately learns. Advances in this area of neuroscience provide educators with insight into the science of learning, and as such, the science behind how design empowers learning.

Advances in learning sciences make apparent the need for "fluid" and "flexible" spaces, whereas classroom spaces, traditionally, have primarily been "fixed." *Fixed spaces* are those in which day after day, lesson after lesson, the design of the learning space primarily remains unchanged. Besides a few 90^0 movements, student desks remain primarily in the same location with the teacher desk seemingly being fastened to the floor. In these spaces student learning most often occurs by listening first, then by doing. In many cases, the "doing" is limited, and a regurgitation-based methodology reigns supreme. In these teacher-centric environments, the design remains virtually the same, regardless of the desired learning experience, as the unilateral space remains fixed, while the content and desired learning outcomes change.

In *fluid and flexible spaces*, as the desired learning outcomes change, so too does the space in which the learning occurs. In these spaces, the design is driven by the learning lens and experience of each individual (see Figure 4.2).

Essential Question: *Does your learning space match your desired pedagogy?*

If we are to design innovative, learner-centric spaces, it's vital to understand what the evidence shows about how design impacts learning. Redesigning learning spaces is about understanding how design impacts the brain and learning; not about being pretty for Pinterest. So then, what are the factors that impact a student's response to their environment?

> Redesigning learning spaces is about understanding how design impacts the brain and learning; not about being pretty for Pinterest.

Driver	Fixed Spaces	Fluid and Flexible Spaces
	As learning outcomes change, the design remains constant.	*The design is driven by the learning experience.*
Common Pedagogy	- Stand and deliver - Consumption-based - Teacher-centric	- Collaborative, project-based, passion-based, or inquiry-based - Learner-centric
Evidence	- Teaching primarily occurs in one large zone - Learning is often passive - Minimal options for seating - Heavy furniture that is difficult to move - Students spend the most amount of time listening or working independently - Most assessments are standardized - Teacher leads most of the conversation	- Teaching occurs in various zones throughout the space - Learning is often active - Various options for seating - Lightweight furniture that can be easily moved - Students spend the most amount of time having conversation or working collaboratively - Assessments are often hands-on and authentic - Students lead most of the conversation

FIGURE 4.2

Understanding How Design Impacts the Brain

In one of the best known studies on the impact of learning-space design, Barrett and colleagues (2015) visited 153 classrooms in 27 different schools, covering rural, suburban, and urban locations. The study analyzed three dimensions of learning-space design: 1. *naturalness* (lighting, air quality, and temperature); 2. *individualization* (flexibility and student ownership); and 3. *stimulation* (appropriate level of). If we are going to design learner-centered, innovative spaces, it's important to understand the design impact of each dimension, so that research can inform our practices.

Naturalness (Lighting, Air Quality, and Temperature)

The notion of "naturalness" design parameters, such as lighting, air quality, and temperature are all important when working to create optimal conditions for learning. In some schools, teachers have minimal control over these areas, and may be limited to large fluorescent lights that are wired in one large zone and are either off or on, no temperature control, and a minimal amount of windows that can be used to provide fresh air into the space. In other classrooms, teachers are able to use various levels of lighting including maximizing natural light, have proper HVAC, and local temperature controls. Regardless of the position teachers find themselves in, it's important that they are aware of the research behind the understanding of how the brain responds to its environment so that they can maximize possibilities in the existing space.

Lighting

Walk into a well-lit room and how do you feel? Contrast that with how you feel after spending a significant part of your day indoors, with minimal access to natural light. Evidence has proven the impact of natural light on the brain, and it's more than its ability to aid sight. Simply put, the more natural light we can have enter the classroom, the better – with one exception: If the natural light becomes a glare, it will have a negative impact.

Practical Tips

◆ Minimize or avoid displays on windows to maximize natural lighting.
◆ Avoid placing large items against areas that block natural light.
◆ Use blinds to minimize glare only; otherwise keep them open.
◆ Design with an "outside-in" approach by utilizing plants and natural color tones similar to nature.
◆ Minimize fluorescent lighting by using lamps to create "warm" lighting, especially in small group areas such as reading nooks.
◆ Utilize outdoor spaces to maximize naturalness.

Air Quality

Poor air quality is a common problem in today's schools, particularly in older spaces. This area is one in which teachers understandably feel they have minimal control, yet evidence shows the impact of air quality on health, attendance, and ultimately learning. Thus teachers should be cognizant of its importance and work to maximize any possible supports.

Practical Tips

◆ Open windows when possible to bring outside air in.
◆ Avoid obstructing open window spaces.
◆ Open classroom doors to provide a pathway for air movement.
◆ In spaces with minimal air movement, use fans to keep air moving throughout the space.
◆ Avoid heavily scented air fresheners.

Temperature

The impact of temperature on learning has been studied for decades. Simply put, students (and the teacher) work more efficiently and effectively in cooler temperatures. As the temperature and humidity in a classroom space rise, students and the teacher feel the effects – attention spans decrease and task performance deteriorates.

Practical Tips

◆ If local control is feasible, maintain a cool temperature.
◆ If local control is not feasible, maximize airflow across the space.
◆ Encourage students to dress in layers to help them control their own comfort levels.
◆ Implement common sense dress code policies.

Other factors

When designing your space, other aspects of "naturalness" should be accounted for such as sound and connections to nature, both of which are secondary factors evident in the research. As such, in an effort to design innovative spaces, the more learning spaces can resemble various aspects of nature, and engage one's senses, the better the brain will respond.

Individualization (Flexibility and Student Ownership)

Thinking back to one's first set of education courses, most educators have studied Maslow's Hierarchy of Needs (1943), a visual description from the 1940s that described five different kinds of human needs (see Figure 4.3). Beginning with the foundation of *physiological* needs such as food and shelter, then followed by *safety*, the next is *love/belonging*, then *esteem*, and finally the highest level of *self-actualization*, the hierarchy visually depicts a series of layers that must be in place for a person to be at their best. The four basic layers of the pyramid contain what Maslow referred to as "deficiency needs," meaning that if a person does not have these in place (physiological, safety, love/belonging, and esteem), the individual will be anxious and unable to focus on secondary, high-level needs.

As we transfer this commonly accepted psychological understanding to the design of learning spaces, the notion of *individualization* from the research becomes apparent. The more students feel as if they belong in the space, the more their brain is ready for higher levels of learning. Therefore, innovative learning-space design is not simply about the physical layout of the classroom, but about understanding how design impacts the brain. As it relates to individualization in this area, flexibility and student ownership are key.

Flexibility

One of the major aspects of designing learner-centered spaces is the ability to adapt the environment in a timely, seamless fashion

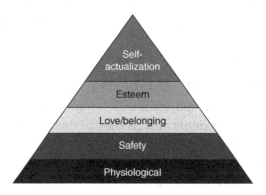

FIGURE 4.3

to meet the desired pedagogy. Since "flexible furniture" has become a trendy topic in recent years, focusing on the why is imperative. Creating flexible spaces is about student agency and choice, not simply about having visually appealing furniture. Flexible "breakout spaces," or zones for smaller group instruction were found to have a positive impact on learning, more so inside a given space than when outside of the main classroom space. Therefore, the notion of "zones," should be used when designing innovative spaces.

Practical Tips

♦ Create "learning zones" for different types of experiences inside your space.
♦ The younger the student, the larger the need for well-defined zones (carpet area, reading nook, etc.).
♦ Be creative with storage spaces and maximize unutilized storage space throughout the building.
♦ Ask students for constructive feedback.

Student Ownership

To learn, students need to feel a sense of belonging, and the personalization of space is an important aspect of one's identity and self-worth. When students feel ownership over the space, and thus a sense of belonging, they will academically perform at higher levels. Personalizing the space, giving students "their" space in a classroom, highlighting and celebrating student work, and recognizing students as individuals, all with their own gifts and abilities, are imperative aspects to designing innovative spaces.

Practical Tips

♦ Ensure cultural diversity in images and artifacts throughout all spaces of the classroom and school.
♦ Highlight students and recognize them as individuals, in various ways throughout the classroom.
♦ Celebrate student work, including that from the arts.
♦ Allow students to personalize artifacts (desk lockers, name drawers, coat spaces, etc.) where appropriate.

◆ Ensure the space is "gender neutral," so both male and female students feel comfortable in their environment.
◆ Construct socially catalytic areas, where relationship building is encouraged.
◆ Ask for constructive feedback from those of the opposite gender and different cultural backgrounds to your own.

Scenarios for Practical Individualization

To understand the practical impact of individualization evident in the research, consider the following fictional, yet very realistic scenarios.

Paisley, a grade 3 student, has her first male teacher of her young educational career. His room is "decorated" in sports motifs and is very masculine in nature. Paisley doesn't like sports and prefers activities such as art and music. Her favorite color is pink.

Caden, a kindergarten student, has a new first year female teacher who loves pink, purple, and polka dots. Her classroom space is therefore saturated with these colors and patterns. Caden says he "doesn't like girl stuff" and prefers "boy stuff" like trucks and sports. His favorite colors are blue and red.

Kelechi moves to a suburban school district in a new state after his father's promotion at work. He enters grade 8 in a school where most students are white and come from different cultural backgrounds, as he is of Nigerian descent and a practicing Muslim. During the months of December and January, Christmas decorations are scattered throughout his classroom space. The teacher says that it is her "favorite holiday." Later in the school year, there is no mention of Eid al-Fitr, an important holiday to mark the end of Ramadan, the Islamic holy month of fasting. Over the year, there is no evidence of respect for his faith, nor is it celebrated as Christmas was for his classmates.

Although fictional in nature, these scenarios, or ones like them, occur regularly in classrooms throughout the world. When designing learning spaces, it's vital to understand the impact of brief or subtle messaging, whether intentional or not, as well as our own personal biases, and what they can signal to students of the opposite gender, another race, or those with religious or cultural differences from our own. The thought that they may be evaluated based on their race or gender can raise fears of confirming negative stereotypes about their group's abilities, and can impact a student's sense of belonging, and thus ultimately their achievement (Steele et al., 2002).

Stimulation (Visual Complexity and Color)

As a principal, I spent a significant amount of time in classrooms. I can specifically remember walking into some early elementary spaces and having to bob and weave around all of the things hanging from the ceiling. Looking around some classroom spaces, every square inch of wall space was utilized, being covered by a poster or something the students had completed that year. I used to think it was a cozy and inviting space, in part because my teachers were incredible. However, at the time, I was naive as regards to the impact of those types of spaces on the brain: Visual complexity can be overstimulating for students, and a distraction for learning.

Visual Complexity

On the whole, in spaces where "visual noise" is the norm, students are off-task more frequently, and off-task for longer periods of time, than in environments where such visual noise is minimal. The converse is also true. Yet extremely low levels of stimulation can also produce poorer learning conditions. Thus a balance is needed.

Practical Tips

- ◆ Focus on learning artifacts, not decorations.
- ◆ Wall displays should be well designed and intentional, not chaotic or outdated.
- ◆ Remove clutter: If it's not being used for instruction, question its purpose.
- ◆ Design to be organized, not chaotic.
- ◆ Avoid placing displays where daylight enters the space.

Color

The impact of color on the brain has been studied at length and can be seen all around us wherever we go. One common example is how such "purposeful intentions" can be seen heavily in the marketing of large companies. Why is it that some companies choose the colors that they do for their brand, while others choose from a very different palette? Take a moment to reflect on the examples given in Figure 4.4.

In analyzing the company brands alongside the psychology behind the colors used, why do you believe the companies listed in Figure 4.4 chose the colors that they did? What are the companies trying to visually communicate about their brand? What types of companies would want to be seen as bold and innovative, while others as calming and trustworthy? Why might a company use warm versus cool colors? What we do know is that these companies are very intentional about their visual messaging because today's largest companies spend billions of dollars each year on advertising and marketing. Just as large companies are intentional in their use of color, educators should also be cognizant of their color choices, due to the impact on people's emotions and perceptions.

Color	Purposeful Intention	Company Logos
Black	Authority, power, strength, intelligence	Apple, Gucci, *New York Times*, Sony
Blue	Calm, trustworthy, honest, secure, focused	Facebook, GE, Ford, American Express
Red	Passionate, action, love, energy, bold	Coca-Cola, Pinterest, Disney, Red Bull, Target
Orange	Happy, friendly, energetic, comfort	Nickelodeon, Home Depot, Nike, Dunkin' Donuts
Green	Natural, fresh, organic, earth, health	Starbucks, Whole Foods, Subway, John Deere
Multicolor	Positive, playful, bold, boundless	Microsoft, Google, eBay, NBC, Instagram

FIGURE 4.4

Practical Tips

◆ Use calming colors in instructional spaces, yet complement with flashes of color (e.g., desks, chairs, etc.).
◆ Avoid creating a "whitewashed" space similar to a sterile hospital environment.
◆ Use bold colors in spaces such as hallways, stairways, etc., or as a classroom accent wall.
◆ Remain "gender neutral" in color choice and design.

Planning for Design Impact

So what was the conclusion from one of the most comprehensive studies on the effects of these areas? In the spaces studied, optimizing each of these physical characteristics improved academic outcomes in math, reading, and writing by 16 percent (Barrett et al., 2015). Of that improvement, the personalization of classrooms, including the notion of flexibility and student choice, accounted for one-fourth of the improvement. It's important to note that each of these areas do not have an equal effect. The breakdown of impact concluded in the study is summarized in Figure 4.5.

> **Essential Question:** *How will research on learning-space design impact your practice moving forward?*

Based on our own everyday experiences, it's hard to deny the impact of our surroundings on our mood, comfort levels, emotion, and willingness to participate in the task at hand. It's also important to maintain a "common sense mindset" throughout the

	Design Factor	*Academic Improvement (%)*
Naturalness	Lighting	21
	Air Quality	16
	Temperature	12
Individualization	Flexibility	17
	Student Ownership	11
Stimulation	Visual Complexity	12
	Color	11

FIGURE 4.5
Source: Barrett et al. (2015)

design and change process. As a teacher and a principal, I served in a 50-year-old building that had no air conditioning, few fresh-air possibilities, and was surrounded by heat-radiating blacktop. That was our reality. However, in serving our students, we must maintain our focus on the things we *can* do, and not harp on those things that are out of our circle of control. Understanding the importance of gender and cultural sensitivity, the advantages to avoiding visual noise, the opportunities that arise in creating learning zones, and the inclusion of student voice in the design process, are only a handful of ways to make changes regardless of the furniture available, budget, or age of the space. A few small changes can make a world of difference and many times it's overcoming our own mindset, which can be our largest obstacle. Our kids need and deserve a can-do type of mindset.

Intentional Design

Learning spaces are the nonverbal story of your school. – Dr. Robert Dillon (Hare and Dillon, 2016)

As we work to create learner-centered classrooms, and focus on the why, it's important that we avoid trendy ideas, unless they are grounded in evidence and are shown favor by students. Learning-space design is about creating the optimal conditions today's learners need to thrive academically. Being *intentional* with our design is key.

> Learning-space design is about creating the optimal conditions today's learners need to thrive academically.

Active Learning, Not Passive Consumption

What type of learning experiences do your students engage in most? Is it primarily *passive consumption*, where the teacher uses a stand-and-deliver methodology and students regurgitate content to demonstrate understanding? Or, are learning experiences more active, where students engage in hands-on experiences, deep conversations, and work collaboratively to create and design? Today's modern learners need the latter, where learning is personal, authentic, and has deep meaning. Consider the following

FIGURE 4.6
Source: Joseph DiPuma, Flagler County Schools, Florida

redesign rendering of an active classroom space located in Flagler County Schools in Florida, as shown in Figure 4.6. What do you notice about the space? Why do you think the space was designed in this way?

What type of learning experiences do you envision happening here? What do you think students would think about such a space? Consider the following:

◆ The space is learner-focused; various zones allow for different types of conversation and collaboration.
◆ Flexibility allows for learners to work together, or to spread apart and work as individuals.
◆ There are a variety of seating options: moveable chairs that are a part of a group, chairs to be used to work quietly as an individual or to move to be part of a group, and seats with a comfortable top.
◆ The room is designed to have students at the front, not the teacher.

◆ The furniture is intentionally fluid and flexible. Moving from one activity to another and rearranging the zones would take little time and effort and could be completed by the students.
◆ Flexible and maneuverable writing surfaces are readily available for student use.
◆ There is little clutter; visual noise is reduced to a minimum.

As we design for active experiences in learning spaces, making items easy to move is key. This enables fluid and quick transitions from group work to individual reflection, and back again. Although realistically not an option in some locations with some furniture, school districts like Flagler County are repurposing tables and chairs by adding low-cost wheels to make the spaces fluid and to help the space be driven by the desired learning outcomes, not by outdated furniture.

Flexible and Affordable

Flexible spaces are complex, living systems that are altered regularly. Side by side, learning spaces that are intentionally designed will rarely appear the same. Walk into one of these spaces and you'll regularly see students moving from one space to the next, creating a different learning zone from the previous activity, adjusting the lights, or reshuffling things around them to suit their personal preferences and needs. Such innovative, learner-centered spaces empower student agency and a sense of control, thus altering their sense of ownership. This fundamentally changes the learning paradigm.

The success in flexibility mirrors a change in instructional pedagogy. Spending money on new flexible furniture is pointless if the stand-and-deliver methodology will remain paramount. However, flexible spaces can alter the fundamental dynamics of student learning experiences, and ultimately empower students to have more agency in their learning, improve active engagement on higher-level tasks, and obliterate the traditional sit-down-and-face-forward orientation of decades past.

Designing innovative spaces is far easier if the money exists to support it. However, the reality is that many, if not most, districts don't have the budget available to purchase new furniture, much less at scale. Thus when redesigning spaces, affordability and sustainability must always remain part of the conversation. As previously shared in this chapter, there are many things that can be done for little to no money when we alter our mindset and become aware of the research on visual messaging, clutter, etc. Educators are some of the most creative problem solvers on the planet, as many continue to develop cost-saving hacks to create dynamic spaces for kids. What are some cost-saving hacks?

Leverage student talents: Partner with your middle or high school vocational or technology education programs to engage students in building what is needed at a minimal cost.

Build community relationships: Contact local big box stores such as Home Depot and build a relationship with the manager. Explain the needs for your classroom or school and ask to be notified about clearance specials, previous displays, or minimally damaged items that they can no longer use.

Ask (plead!) for help: Every day on social media, teachers are seen sharing donations they have received, grants that were funded, or support from their local community. Be the largest possible advocate for your students' needs, and watch what can happen.

Repurpose what you currently have: School districts like Flagler County in Florida are repurposing old tables by painting on writable surfaces, replacing standard table legs with those that are mobile, and adding fresh coats of paint to make the old new once again.

Find "classroom hacks" online: Search "iPad storage hacks" or "classroom storage hacks" online to find innovative ideas that have been put into practice, yet cost little to create or implement.

Make small spaces count: Consider creating small, collaborative areas of innovation, especially in non-traditional areas that are often overlooked or under-utilized. Often called "watering holes," "campfires," or "caves," these micro-spaces can leverage small square-footage for large impact.

Spaces to Create, Design, and Tinker

> If you build it, they will come, and if you let them build it, they will learn. – Laura Fleming (2018)

Inspiring wonder, provoking curiosity, and empowering students to design, create, and tinker are vital components in meeting the needs of today's learners. From a small, individual space in the corner of a classroom, to a section of the library, to a full scale room, empowering students with such opportunities isn't just one of the latest fads; it's a research-based method to shift the learning culture of a school community.

In the first in-depth examination of K–12 education makerspaces, Kim and colleagues (2018) revealed the significance of cultural aspects of making (*student interests, real-world relevance,* and *community collaboration*) to empower learning. The research underlined how makerspaces can foster a range of positive student learning outcomes. The report also highlighted some longstanding equity issues common in the STEM (Science, Tech, Engineering, and Math) fields related to gender, race, and socioeconomic status.

After this report was completed, the ExCITe Center at Drexel University made the following recommendations (Kim et al., 2018):

♦ The culture of a makerspace has a direct impact on student learning. Rather than choosing equipment or specific projects, designers of new makerspaces should first consider the kind of learning culture they seek to create for their students.

♦ Makerspace participation can positively impact a broad range of students, including English Language learners. But school leaders must be mindful to recruit inclusively, for both the instructors and students.

♦ Within school makerspaces, hosting unstructured open hours (outside of class time) encourages greater exploration, positive risk taking, and collaboration for a wider range of students.

♦ Students frequently use skills learned in makerspaces to improve other aspects of the school and local community, such as student government activities, classroom maintenance, and sports facilities.

As highlighted in the report, these types of high-level learning experiences have traditionally been lacking for our females, students of color, or those not at the top of their class. Quite often, these opportunities are reserved for those labeled "gifted," those on honor roll, or those who have previously excelled in other areas. Such biased structures have created large equity gaps, depriving groups of students who could benefit the most from these types of learning experiences. Therefore, it's vital that educators actively recruit a diverse set of students when these types of experiences are optional, and ideally, find ways to ensure equity in opportunity. When intentionally designing these types of learning experiences, ensuring equity means opportunities for *all* students.

Essential Question: *How will you ensure equity in opportunity for the learners that you serve?*

> Creating such functional and equitable spaces that inspire tinkering and creation isn't about throwing LEGOs at students and hoping they learn something.

Creating such functional and equitable spaces that inspire tinkering and creation isn't about throwing LEGOs at students and hoping they learn something. Effective makerspaces are intentionally designed to promote higher order thinking, reflection, creation, inquiry, deductive reasoning, and design skills. One such makerspace can be found in Flagler County Schools (see Figure 4.7). Here, school leaders wanted to create a space that offered the resilience and freedom necessary for students to follow their interests and passions and to do so collaboratively and progressively. They believed that to successfully inspire students to engage their deepest ambitions in a creative, productive fashion, they needed to make learning personal. To do so, they knew a personalized learning environment was needed to match the desired learning outcomes and ultimately bring the experience to life.

This vision for student learning became realized when The Nexus of Engineering, Science, and Technology, known as "The NEST," was created. The purpose behind The NEST was to establish a presence of basic, structural, and virtual

FIGURE 4.7
Source: Joseph DiPuma, Flagler County Schools, Florida

engineering by utilizing an abundance of maker-tools powered by a dynamic, project-based approach that aligned teaching and learning strategies in a direction that ensured positive outcomes and student achievement; all the while supporting a dynamic school learning culture. Joseph DiPuma, the district technology and innovation coordinator in Flagler County Schools, explains:

> It's true, The NEST is unique in many ways, but what we really love is the cultural impact it's had on our learners. From the moment students enter, they're cloaked with ambition, drive, curiosity, and the need to create and discover. It's vital that they feel empowered and energized by new things and we need environments that can cultivate and supercharge their creativeness while unmasking the "sorcery" behind the functionality of technological things. We must also relay the impression that failure is ok as long as success is imminent.
>
> DiPuma (2018)

> When we empower today's learners to follow their interests and passions, while simultaneously leveraging real-world, hands-on, deeper learning experiences, anything becomes possible.

As educators, we must unleash the vast array of talent found in every one of our students. When we empower today's learners to follow their interests and passions, while simultaneously leveraging real-world, hands-on, deeper learning experiences, anything becomes possible. Providing students with innovative, learner-centered spaces to tinker and create is one conduit to bring such experiences to reality.

Conclusion

Today, researchers continue to make great strides in the science of learning. As we learn more about the complexity of the human brain and how to create optimal learning conditions for functionality, the notion of learning-space redesign moves far past some trendy idea, to one of necessity. Aligning our space with our desired learning outcomes moves from something that's nice to have, to a foundational component of driving successful learning outcomes.

Each space, whether old or new, large or small, should be designed to maximize a personal approach to deep levels of student learning. Schools will know that their spaces have been designed successfully when the design positively contributes to the learning process and helps create an authentic, dynamic experience for *all* students (Sheninger and Murray, 2017).

For educators who are unsure of where to start, begin by taking one step. What's a common space in your classroom or school that could benefit all students? How could the space better be designed to be innovative and learner-centered? How can we increase the space for learning by decreasing the traditional teacher footprint? Most importantly, what do students think about the need to change or changes that have occurred? Understanding that there is not one "right way" is vital as the design of the space should take into consideration the unique characteristics of the school's community and the talented students that it serves. As we model our own learning to students, we cannot be afraid to fail forward, as such transformation takes time.

As we work to redesign our spaces, we must remain hyperfocused on our why and understand that simply placing new furniture and colorful beanbags into a space will not in and of itself improve student learning outcomes. It's the dynamic, innovative use of the learning space by the teacher and students that maximizes the impact on learning. Therefore, simply rearranging your classroom space will have little to no impact on learning outcomes if the instructional design and pedagogy don't evolve along with it. Shifting pedagogy to focus on personal and authentic learning opportunities that leverage flexible and fluid spaces to maximize possibilities is ultimately the difference maker.

> Therefore, simply rearranging your classroom space will have little to no impact on learning outcomes if the instructional design and pedagogy don't evolve along with it.

Let us never forget that our top priority is about loving and caring for the students that we have the privilege to serve. Everything else is secondary. Every day that we are with students is an opportunity to do something amazing and to show them how much they matter. Together, let's design the innovative, learner-centered spaces that our kids need. It will show them that the work we do is not about us, but is all about them. Take one step and then another. Together, we can do this.

References

Barrett, P., Zhang, Y., Davies, F., and Barrett, L. (2015, February). Clever Classrooms: Summary Report of the HEAD Project (Holistic Evidence and Design). Accessed October 9, 2018: www.salford.ac.uk/cleverclassrooms/1503-Salford-Uni-Report-DIGITAL.pdf

DiPuma, J. (2018, July 10). RE: Learning Spaces Chapter. Personal Communication (Email).

Fleming, L. (2018). The Kickstart Guide to Making Great Makerspaces. Thousand Oaks, CA: Corwin.

Hare, R. L. and Dillon, R. (2016). *The Space: A Guide for Educators*. Irvine, CA: EdTechTeam Press.

Kim, Y., Edouard, K., Alderfer, K., and Smith, B. (2018). Making Culture: A National Study of Education Makerspaces. Accessed October 9, 2018: http://drexel.edu/excite/engagement/learning-innovation/making-culture-report/

Maslow, A. H. (1943). "A theory of human motivation." *Psychological Review*, 50(4), 370–96.

Sheninger, E. and Murray, T. (2017). *Learning Transformed: 8 Keys to Designing Tomorrow's Schools, Today*. Alexandria, VA: ASCD.

Sinek, S. (2009). *Start With Why: How Great Leaders Inspire Everyone to Take Action*. New York: Portfolio.

Steele, C. M., Spencer, S. J., and Aronson, J. (2002). "Contending with group image: The psychology of stereotype and social identity threat." *Advances in Experimental Social Psychology*, 34, 379–440.

5

Innovative Assessment that Amplifies Student Voice

Starr Sackstein

Four distinct student personalities sit around a table, reviewing old lesson plans and projects. Thumbing through objectives, conferring, and deciding together about what their potential learning experience could look like. This isn't the first time they've contributed to learning decisions, but it is the first time they have had the opportunity to design their own learning from scratch, the way their teachers have always done for them.

Learning simply can't be dictated by the single person in charge of the classroom. Since each room is made up of a variety of moving parts, each one of the individuals who make up the collective whole must be invested in the everyday happenings. And the longer the teacher is in the classroom, the farther he or she gets from the experience of being a student.

Innovative educators consider their learners first and break the mold of how it has always been. They change with the needs of those who make up the genetics of the space. They invest in possible learning even if the possibilities haven't existed before. They ask questions without the fear of being wrong. They take risks. They reinvent what has always been done to truly challenge and inspire relevant progress in each of the learners. They are reflective and deeply courageous. They matter. Everyone in their classroom matters.

Set up a Student-Centered Learning Environment

> For really excellent student learning to occur, it is essential to build the right conditions for the students in it. These routines and protocols will take a lot of front loading but will be rewarded in the long run.

For really excellent student learning to occur, it is essential to build the right conditions for the students in it. These routines and protocols will take a lot of front loading but will be rewarded in the long run, so take your time in the beginning and never underestimate the power of building relationships with the people who will be learning in this space. Additionally, remember that you aren't just establishing rapport for teacher to student; you also have to be sure to develop learning relationships between students.

Let's face it; no one is going to take a risk, even one as small as raising his or her hand if he or she doesn't feel safe to do it. So it is incumbent upon the educator in the room to create a learning space that is both nurturing and somewhat predictable. Here are some steps a teacher can take to make sure the classroom is primed and ready for innovative learning:

♦ **Get to know all of your learners early.** Ice breaking activities can ensure that while you are learning about your students, they are learning about each other. One example is a "Find Someone Who" activity that allows students to move around the room, mixing and networking with each other, as they ask low-stakes questions and figure out things about each other. This activity can be followed up by a short writing assignment that allows them to interview a partner in greater depth and write a profile about that learner. These profiles can then be shared in presentation. The end to the activity can be a bulletin board of photos with a memorable quote under each face and name.

- ◆ **Students set goals publicly and they are visible throughout the year.** One year I made a cloud wall with student goals and as they met their learning targets, they were able to take down the goal and replace it with another one. Keeping learning visible keeps everyone accountable.
- ◆ **Establish guidelines with students about non-negotiables for the learning environment.** This will give the educator an opportunity to hear what students need to feel safe in a learning environment. Some classes may want to write some kind of document that can be hung on an anchor chart or a simple list of expectations. These will generally include, but are not limited to: Respect each other, listen to everyone's voice, positively enforce actions that promote being an upstander, and try one's best. The list of non-negotiables should be no more than five items. Less is more when it comes to "rules."
- ◆ **Consistently enforce non-negotiables so that all students are clear on expectations.** Students should be involved in the making of consequences so that they understand the implications of breaking a non-negotiable. For this to work well, the teacher must make sure all students are treated equitably. Students may even be empowered to help maintain the safe learning environment. It should be a collective buy-in for best outcomes.
- ◆ **Value each child and what he or she brings to the learning environment.** All children will have something different to contribute and the teacher needs to make sure to highlight, acknowledge, and praise those assets when they support the learning space. A specific piece of feedback or a sticker for a job well done goes a long way to showing students you recognize their contributions.
- ◆ **Model making mistakes and be transparent about growing from them.** At some point in a child's life, guessing and being wrong becomes a scary proposition. I suspect it is when schools start testing. Prior to this time, students actively answer questions and keep trying until they get to the "right" answer. As adults, we

must be intentional and transparent about our mistakes. So in class, when we make a mistake, we must promptly acknowledge it, name it, and work out a solution together. Sometimes this will happen after class ends, so it is important to make sure you don't just let it slide. Find a way to build it into the next lesson. Call the class's attention to the misinformation or any other mistake and present it as a learning opportunity for everyone.

> If we want students to feel safe and take risks, we must create an ideal learning space that encourages and supports the constructive behaviors, and values mistakes and learning opportunities.

Ultimately, if we want students to feel safe and take risks, we must create an ideal learning space that encourages and supports the constructive behaviors, and values mistakes and learning opportunities. There are many times in the classroom that I misspoke or shared information that I believed to be correct when it wasn't. It never felt great to be challenged by a student at first, but in this age of mobile technology, what a great teaching moment. Rather than pretend I know everything, it works much better to say, "You know what?, I don't know the answer to that question. Let's figure it out together." In this way students know that we are all learners, no matter how old or how educated and that it is essential to make mistakes to grow.

Transparently Embed Standards throughout Lessons

Standards are not innately known by our learners. Sometimes they are not even known by the professionals in the room. If we want students to know how to talk about their learning in a meaningful way, we must first give them the vocabulary to be able to understand what they are learning.

The best way to introduce standards is by helping students understand the difference between skills and content knowledge, and then starting each lesson with a clear *learning target* (or objective, or aim, or whatever clever term you call it in your school). Make sure the learning intention is clear, visible, and connected to what they are actually doing in the work period. Also make sure that it doesn't encompass too much; a good learning target should be focused and easy to recognize for students.

The language of standards is not always accessible, so it is important to help students make sense of these important expectations. If educators do this briefly in every class period at the beginning, students become accustomed to hearing the language and understand why they are doing the work they are. This also helps them communicate what they know, in a language that aligns with how they will likely be assessed.

Since the ultimate goal of innovative student-designed assessment is putting the onus on the learner to help develop the task, students need to be able to articulate and build what and why they are doing it. Too often the tasks and/or projects we design for assessment aren't robust enough or aligned with standards, and therefore aren't excellent opportunities to show growth and learning.

Another way to help students engage with the standards is to ask them to jigsaw them in small groups. Ask them to rewrite the standards for the particular unit being taught and keep the student-written standards hanging on the wall as an anchor to the work. Always reference their rewrites and when it comes time to start designing their own work, they will know what objectives they are working toward. Sentence strips are awesome for rewriting standards. If a unit covers five standards, give one standard to each group. Have them read it and then rewrite it. They could even come up with different assignments they have done that demonstrate this standard from the past as examples. This, too, will be helpful when it comes time for them to design their own standards.

Make sure to keep the current standards clearly displayed in the room for regular reference. The more embedded they are in the learning process, the more students will internalize them. To truly be able to do the work we want them to do, we can't simply affix standards after the fact, we must build them in, connect with them, and build from them all of the time: In this way, students will become adept at using them while creating learning experiences and reflecting on those experiences.

Build Student-Designed Learning Experiences

Educators understand that there is curricula to be taught and standards to be mastered. We are the experts of this content and often hoard that experience for ourselves, since we are the professionals, of course. This will always be true, but that doesn't mean that students shouldn't or can't be involved in the learning design process. The teacher will have to determine the appropriate time to start scaffolding student voice into this process. It will vary from class to class and with age, depending on student readiness. Some will be able to participate sooner than others and that is normal. Know your students and take the time to appropriately group them as you begin the student-designed learning process, the five steps of which are now outlined.

> **Use a framework:** Teachers should *always* start with a framework. Students should be aware of this framework, starting with the end in mind. This way, teachers and students can work together toward the same end goal, building on earlier experiences they've had when the teachers designed the learning for them.

Early in the year, when the teacher is modeling how to design assessments, he or she needs to be intentional and transparent in what the assessment is for. Starting with a backward design approach, as a class we can look at a project and determine what skills will be necessary for success. For example, in my English class, I would share an electronic document with the assignment on it. Students would be asked to read and annotate, first alone and then in small groups, noting areas of question and areas for connection. "What is the purpose of this assignment?" I may ask, or "What might you need to be successful?" Students would then be asked to think about what they know already and what they need to be taught.

As the students share out, either verbally or written, the teacher notes what needs to be taught. These discussions will be the genesis for mini-lessons and small group instruction based on needs. This keeps learning solidly within the students' needs and goals, and invites them into the process of learning design, even if they aren't ready to participate in creating a project yet.

Know student strengths: As mentioned earlier, getting to know students early in the year is important, paying close attention to the kind of learners all students are by providing a plethora of activities that activate learning in different ways. Students should be able to articulate the mode of learning that highlights their strengths. We can do this by being transparent when we are doing the lessons. For example, today we are going to be doing a stations activity that will allow you to be kinesthetic, collaborative, and creative, depending on the station you are engaging with. After the experience, students can then reflect not only on the learning they did, but the experience itself. Was this an activity that leant itself readily to their best learning style?

Provide teacher examples: Using teacher written assignments as a model, students can work in groups, pairs, or alone to design learning experiences. Teachers should provide many examples for analysis when beginning this process. Ask students to annotate and discover what they notice about these different learning experiences. How are they worded? What do they look like? What are they assessing? How might they do it differently? Make sure to provide a variety of examples that show both good assignments and weaker ones. Students should be able to identify the differences and articulate the reasons for effectiveness, as this will be a key piece in their building their own learning experiences.

Give choices: When first bringing students into the process, teachers may want to start with choices for students to pick their own assignments. Not just a choice in content, but also a choice in process and product. Give them ideas about what it could look like and let them choose. Help the students to be able to create their own learning experiences. Some students will have ideas right away: Practice saying yes with these students. Walk through the experience with them and they will become valuable assets later when they are working among the groups of students doing it for the first time without the teacher's help.

Figure 5.1 shows an example of offering choice to the students when designing their own learning experiences. The assignment sheet for "Choose Your Own Adventure" is set up in parts, so that students can select from different choices in order to build the whole assignment from scratch.

Mixed Media – Final Project – Choose your own adventure

This year you will be selecting and creating your own final assessment. You will create your assignment, the format in which you want to present it, and the content you want to work with related to journalism.

Phase 1 – Selecting a topic and/or mode to do the project in. **Due 4/24**

Column A – Topics	Column B – Mode
Journalism ethics	Investigative feature
Photojournalism	Photo essay
Coverage of any major event	Series of short form pieces
Journalism history	Podcast
Technology	Video
	Scrapbook/yearbook style

FIGURE 5.1

Create banks of activities/resources: After students are accustomed to making solid learning choices that work to their strengths, begin to take off the training wheels. As a whole class, create a bank of different kinds of activities and align them with different learning styles. Give the students the language and the tools to understand why we make the choices we do when designing learning experiences. Let them ask a lot of questions and in turn, ask them a lot of questions about their choices. It's okay to make the students a little uncomfortable because they need to understand the importance of intention when designing these experiences.

At the very least, students will become more empathetic toward their teachers because they will realize how much work goes into a truly well-designed learning experience. It is easily taken for granted because those of us who are really good at it, really pay attention to the details, and the execution seems so easy. Of course, we know that it is really a function of excellent planning, and that takes time and practice.

Once the students have a bank of possible ideas for activities, they can also build resource curations that will help them later. Whether digital texts, books, articles, or videos, students have access to many free resources that will enhance their learning experience. These curated resource lists can be housed electronically for the whole class to use and continuously be added to as new resources are found. Applications and websites like Diigo provide access for shared libraries that allow for annotation and keyword tagging.

Determine Success Criteria Together

It's not enough to bring the students into the design of the learning: They must also be involved in determining success criteria. Over time, they will become adept at giving and receiving feedback in this atmosphere and will therefore have internalized what makes work successful.

When we intentionally design learning, we are always considering what mastery looks like and students should also be able to articulate it. In class, teachers can start with a brainstorming activity that looks at the learning experience and teases out the specific skills being assessed. Then in small groups, students can have collaborative conversations that develop ideas about when you know you've mastered that skill. What does it look like? What will the student's work show? Once students have determined the different skills and what mastery looks like, as a class, we can start to design a standards-aligned rubric that allows some flexibility to students.

> Don't assume that just because a rubric is provided, it is done well. Having random categories like "neatness" or "creativity" with a scale of four that use vague words that don't communicate learning can be counterproductive.

A note of caution about rubrics in general: Don't assume that just because a rubric is provided, it is done well. Having random categories like "neatness" or "creativity" with a scale of four that use vague words that don't communicate learning can be counterproductive. Be sure that the language of the rubric makes sense to the students and is assessing and communicating the learning in a meaningful way.

One method to consider is the single point rubric (see Figure 5.2), where the particular skill with a short description is presented in the middle, and then space is given on both sides for evidence of less or more proficiency. Using this kind of rubric offers students a more authentic assessment communication experience. This can also be a great precursor to self-assessment and reflection if the teacher provides scaffolding questions to help the students better support their discussion of learning. The scaffolded questions can match the standards to help students know what to write and how to evaluate their own work based on these standards.

Not There Yet	Skill or Standard	Meets and/or Exceeds
	Cite specific textual evidence to support analysis of primary and secondary sources, attending to such features as the date and origin of the information. CCSS. ELA-LITERACY.RH.9–10.1	
	Assess the extent to which the reasoning and evidence in a text support the author's claims. CCSS.ELA-LITERACY.RH.9–10.8	

FIGURE 5.2

Another way in which success criteria can be determined is to develop a list of skills and then align them with standards, making sure to discuss what mastery looks like. Examples should be provided. Then students can score themselves out of four (1 = not there yet, 2 = approaching standards, 3 = meets standards, 4 = exceeds standards). It could look like Figure 5.3.

These rubrics will help students articulate their learning and communicate differently about it in language that aligns with the standards.

Know When to Release Control

Perhaps it goes without saying that you won't be starting a completely student-led learning experience in September; it takes some time to build the atmosphere and slowly release control. Doing it too soon will ensure failure and potentially promote ill will with the students. They need to be ready to take on the task, and therefore we have to build their level of readiness in a scaffolded and intentional way.

Depending on the age of your learners, they will come to you with different levels of comfort as regards control. While I was in the classroom, I worked with grade 9 students in my Foundations in Journalism class and with grade 11 and 12 students for the rest of the day. Despite having a range of ages, most of the students hadn't been exposed to this kind of learning prior to me, so it didn't matter that some were 14 and others were 17 years old; it was new for all of them. So we started the same way, with the end in mind.

For the senior students, they received a syllabus with the learning outlined for the entire year, with the caveat that things could change based on the class's needs and pacing would likely be adjusted. Seeing all of the work up front was a little overwhelming at first, but they were always assured that the learning experiences were scaffolded to build confidence and stamina as they prepared for college. Knowing they were ending with a 12–15-page college research paper meant that all the skills we were learning throughout the year were readying them for

Skill	Common Core Standard(s)	Level
Determining the importance of an issue in journalism ethics to center your Pubic Service Announcement (PSA) around	Analyze various accounts of a subject told in different mediums (e.g., a person's life story in both print and multimedia), determining which details are emphasized in each account.	
Understanding the journalism ethics topics inside and out	Determine a central idea of a text and analyze its development over the course of the text, including how it emerges and is shaped and refined by specific details; provide an objective summary of the text.	
	Conduct short as well as more sustained research projects to answer a question (including a self-generated question) or solve a problem; narrow or broaden the inquiry when appropriate; synthesize multiple sources on the subject, demonstrating understanding of the subject under investigation.	
Developing and drawing a storyboard to convey a plan	Write informative/explanatory texts to examine and convey complex ideas, concepts, and information clearly and accurately through the effective selection, organization, and analysis of content.	
	CCSS.ELA-Literacy.W.9–10.2a Introduce a topic; organize complex ideas, concepts, and information to make important connections and distinctions; include formatting (e.g., headings), graphics (e.g., figures, tables), and multimedia when useful to aiding comprehension.	
	CCSS.ELA-Literacy.W.9–10.2b Develop the topic with well-chosen, relevant, and sufficient facts, extended definitions, concrete details, quotations, or other information and examples appropriate to the audience's knowledge of the topic.	
	CCSS.ELA-Literacy.W.9–10.2c Use appropriate and varied transitions to link the major sections of the text, create cohesion, and clarify the relationships among complex ideas and concepts.	

FIGURE 5.3

Skill	Common Core Standard(s)	Level
Assigning roles in the group, so work is distributed evenly	Work with peers to set rules for collegial discussions and decision making (e.g., informal consensus, taking votes on key issues, presentation of alternate views), clear goals and deadlines, and individual roles as needed.	
Using all three basic camera angles in your PSA	Integrate and evaluate information presented in diverse media and formats, including visually, quantitatively, and orally.	
Filming your PSA with an iPhone or flip cam	Use technology, including the internet, to produce, publish, and update individual or shared writing products, taking advantage of technology's capacity to link to other information and to display information flexibly and dynamically.	
Editing your footage with iMovie or Movie Maker	Make strategic use of digital media (e.g., textual, graphical, audio, visual, and interactive elements) in presentations to enhance understanding of findings, reasoning, and evidence, and to add interest.	
Making revisions along the way, as necessary, to make sure you can show your understanding of what a PSA is	Engage and orient the reader by setting out a problem, situation, or observation, establishing one or multiple point(s) of view, and introducing a narrator and/or characters; create a smooth progression of experiences or events.	
	Develop and strengthen writing as needed by planning, revising, editing, rewriting, or trying a new approach, focusing on addressing what is most significant for a specific purpose and audience.	
Setting deadlines and following directions appropriately; asking questions when confused	Propel conversations by posing and responding to questions that relate the current discussion to broader themes or larger ideas; actively incorporate others into the discussion; clarify, verify, or challenge ideas and conclusions.	
Reflecting on your learning based on the standards to show your own knowledge of how and what you have learned	Write routinely over extended time frames (time for research, reflection, and revision) and shorter time frames (a single sitting or a day or two) for a range of tasks, purposes, and audiences.	

FIGURE 5.3 (Cont.)

what was to come, and that was transparently connected all of the time.

For younger students, a more flexible outline was provided, but each unit worked much in the same way as the older students. They knew the final outcome first, and then we worked backward to prepare them for success.

As we were building our culture, expectations were always clear and input from students always accepted. Since they were already aware of the standards and learning was transparent, when the first learning experience arrived we discussed what made it different from the traditional experience. We explored the assignment sheet together and although the teacher had initially structured it, there was flexibility built in immediately. Regardless of the assignment provided, students always had the option to stray and create something of their own.

In our class, the first major project was a group assignment. Through this assignment we set important norms and established classroom routines. Additionally, collaborative skills were taught and enhanced through small group work throughout the week in class. Since the class was run like a workshop, most days there was either a whole class mini-lesson taken from the formative assessments the day before or individual small group mini-lessons based on where an individual group was in the process.

Releasing control of the class is something that a group works through together. Too often teachers worry about releasing control to students for a myriad of reasons, mostly stemming from fear of the unknown or one or two bad experiences. Letting go of control takes practice, much like taking off training wheels and setting a rider free. The rider will undoubtedly fall, and that will be hard for the rider and the watcher, but to learn, the rider must get up and try again because practice is the only way to success.

> Letting go of control takes practice, much like taking off training wheels and setting a rider free. The rider will undoubtedly fall, and that will be hard for the rider and the watcher, but to learn, the rider must get up and try again.

At first, students will also be uncomfortable with this shift in control. They will push back: It's easier for them to do what they are told than it is for them to take ownership of their learning. Perhaps they will buck or sulk or create challenges. Keep pushing forward. Here are some things to look for in class that show signs of readiness for students to take control of their learning:

- ◆ Students who are inherently asking a lot of "why" questions.
- ◆ Students who finish work early and are eager to pursue areas of interest related to the learning.
- ◆ Students exhibiting leadership qualities and confidence in the content area.
- ◆ Students who need more of a challenge that goes beyond a short extension activity.
- ◆ Students who are gripping tightly to protocols but clearly don't need them. Many of these students could be uncomfortable with change; they might just need a pep talk and/or confidence booster.

Provide Feedback Along the Way

Feedback is an integral part of the learning experience and it must be happening throughout the learning process in a variety of different ways. Students can be empowered to maintain this feedback and use it while setting goals and tracking their own progress. These goals can become the lifeline of these experiences. In the same way that we differentiate for students with Individualized Learning Plans (IEPs), allowing students to get the feedback they need based on the goals they set can directly align with student-designed learning experiences.

When teachers model designing learning experiences, they should be actively eliciting feedback from students and providing both constructive and positive feedback directly linked to learning outcomes. The more specific our own questions for feedback are, as well as the action-oriented feedback we provide, the better students will understand the concept of effective feedback (see Figure 5.4).

Feedback Dos	Feedback Don'ts

Do answer student questions with extremely specific answers that provide a strategy for improving whatever needs to be improved. For example, instead of saying "your introductory paragraph needs some work," consider saying something like, "your introductory paragraph has a good claim, but more context building is necessary to bring the reader in. Go back to the notes you took from the lesson on context building." This is also the case when designing student-designed learning experiences: Challenge students to know their why when creating these assignments and ask them to articulate it.

Do encourage students to go to their peers before coming to the teacher for help. The teacher can't be the only person giving feedback in the room. There isn't enough time in the day. So building a culture where students know how to provide excellent feedback is necessary.

Do be a reader/audience for your students, and not just the teacher. Try to view their work through that lens, so you can ask clarifying questions that will lead students to fill gaps and find answers. Let the students be the learners. Some students may need you to direct them toward resources, which you can provide as you go.

Do communicate feedback in multiple ways. There are a lot of great apps out there that can make giving feedback a lot easier. The more often students hear feedback, in a variety of ways, the more adept they become at using it. Try using apps like Voxer for voice feedback. When you have critical feedback to share and can't do it in person, using your voice goes a long way. They can hear nuance that they wouldn't be able to read.

Don't allow students to ask if something is "good." This is a loaded question that can't adequately be answered. You may want to turn it around and tell students to ask more directed questions, so you can understand what they are really asking. Teach them to be specific. For example, if a student hands you an assignment idea and says, "is this good?" You may say, "what exactly would you like me to comment on? The directions? The task itself? Where do you think feedback would be most effective?" Always try to tease it out with the students so they understand the point of what you are asking. They need to make the decisions themselves.

Don't do the work for the students. While giving feedback, don't make corrections without offering opportunities for students to work it through on their own. It is definitely easier to just correct an answer or a sentence, but a student learns nothing from your doing it for them.

Don't mark everything that is "wrong" at once. Focus your feedback. Try not to overwhelm with too much at once. Giving students one to three things to focus on at any given time will offer them opportunities to grow a little at a time, in a way they can manage.

Don't offer empty praise. Even when learning warrants genuine positive praise, be specific in how you offer it. Tell them what works well and more importantly, why, so they can replicate it. Every piece of feedback should be a growing opportunity, even when the learning has been fully grasped. This is also a good opportunity to set new goals. Perhaps this student could be a helper for students who are still developing the skills.

FIGURE 5.4

Ultimately, the feedback we provide for students sets the foundation for what they will be able to provide to each other, and it helps them to predict how well they will grow in terms of their own learning. The better the feedback and the learning conversations, the higher likelihood for substantial progress and self-efficacy.

Promote a Culture of Reflection

Reflection is one of the most essential parts to lifelong learning and it doesn't come naturally to everyone. In order to promote a culture of reflective practice, we must make time for it in class, so students can explore what worked, what didn't work, and where they still need to practice to keep improving.

Reflection can start as small as an exit ticket that explores what was learned in a class period or during a project, as well as determining any misconceptions or challenges that have arisen. Teachers can model this behavior for students at the end of the class period, when they write with students to share what they learned and what they will adjust based on that learning. For example, after taking the status of the class throughout the period and sharing conversations with students in small groups, I may learn that I didn't teach a concept well enough. Perhaps one or two students got it really well and after conferring with these students, as well as the ones that haven't, I may suggest we undertake a "do-over" the next day. More resources will be collected and I will enlist the help of the students who understood it to ensure that everyone else gets it the second time around.

The flexible nature of reflection helps teachers and students consider their own personal growth. This growth is what will fuel future learning as we continue to build foundational skills. Reflection in itself is a foundational skill and an essential one to be taught and practiced in class regularly. The more control we release to students, the more involved they are in the process, and the more they need to think about their learning and provide

> Learning is full of nuances, and since we don't know what is going on in the heads of our students, reflection offers a window into what we can't see.

feedback on it in different ways. Learning is full of nuances, and since we don't know what is going on in the heads of our students, reflection offers a window into what we can't see.

Often we have students who don't participate or engage as much as we would like, and encouraging these students to share reflections whether in writing, or video, or audio, gives them a chance to show what they know even if they haven't completed all of the assignments. We have to catch students in the process, help them document their learning, so when it comes time to assess what they know and can do, we have an adequate amount of evidence to support our understanding of their knowing.

Conclusion

Innovative assessment that amplifies student voice by giving them ownership of every aspect of their learning better prepares the young to be critical adult thinkers. Students will be able to navigate situations without specific directions and will more easily and creatively be able to discover solutions. We owe it to our students to let them bring areas of uncharted learning to the table. Let's challenge students to go deeper than mere comprehension activities and push them straight into creation and synthesis.

6

Innovating the Math Classroom

Kirk Humphreys

Too often when we think of a math classroom, we think of a classroom full of students facing forward and listening to their teacher explain the lesson for the day. If time permits, the teacher allows students to work on problems that are assigned. Any problems not completed by the end of class become homework. Students work through problems at home that mimic those in class. Students sometimes struggle at home on the homework, either not completing the homework or finding answers through friends or family. Students often wait until class the next day to ask questions about the problems they didn't understand on the homework. This pattern repeats itself throughout the school year. Math becomes a struggle for a lot of students.

I, too, followed this model for over a decade. I taught in this traditional method because I knew of nothing else. All through my schooling years the traditional model seemed to work for me. Consequently, I taught using the same methods and it worked for me. At least I thought it did until I realized I had an issue with how much class time was wasted going over questions. I would often start class by reviewing problems from homework that students did not understand. This was time consuming, especially when I only had a 42-minute period. It would not be uncommon to spend upwards of 15 minutes going over problems. Spending this much time on homework meant I had less time to go over the lesson for the day. I knew this was not the best use of my time.

A few weeks earlier I had watched a video on the "flipped" classroom by Jon Bergmann and Aaron Sams (2015). A flipped classroom is a teaching and learning strategy that reverses the traditional learning environment by delivering instructional content, often online, outside of the classroom and then practicing what is learned outside the classroom while in the classroom. Just before the second semester was about to begin, I decided I would radically change my classroom by implementing a flipped classroom. I sent an email out to the parents of my students informing them. It was a huge success. In subsequent years, my pedagogy continued to change and my classroom has morphed into what it is today. While the flipped model has allowed me to innovate my classroom, it isn't the videos that make my classroom effective. It is the time I now have with students to engage them in a classroom environment where they take ownership of their learning.

Over the course of the last few years, I have tried numerous ways to hand over ownership to my students. I have tried out different methods with my students and made changes while we tried them. Students not only are trying out different ways to learn and take ownership but I am also modeling failure and success for them. They see their teacher trying new things and being unafraid to fail. I often tell students that we are trying something new. I always invite feedback from students and then make changes from there to make it the most successful I can. While you are making changes within your own classroom, don't be afraid to fail. Realize that it will take time to change and the suggestions and ideas explained within this chapter are from years of changes within my own classroom. The following chapter represents all of the areas in which significant changes have been made from a traditional math classroom.

> While you are making changes within your own classroom, don't be afraid to fail. Realize that it will take time to change.

Pacing

In a traditional math classroom, teachers often present a new lesson every day. These math teachers want to spend one day on each lesson as they progress through the material. Let's rethink how we can use class time and student choice with pacing, in order to be more flexible.

Students all work through material at a different pace. Within my flipped classroom, students receive the instruction at home. In class, students have time to work on and practice these concepts. The entire unit is laid out ahead of time so students can choose the pace that is comfortable for them. Students are given an end date in which the unit and assessment should be completed. Students plan out their time accordingly, determining when to watch the videos at home and when to do the practice and activities in class. Within one class period, students may be learning at multiple different points within the unit. Giving students choice in their pacing allows them to fully take the time to understand the concepts being learned as well as not having to wait for others who have yet to master the content.

Differences in pacing also allows students to plan around their individual schedules. It provides students with choice over their learning. Students have the opportunity to schedule the unit as they see fit. In addition, if students are absent, it allows them time to catch up with the material learned in class as there is no pace of the class to keep up with. By differing the pacing throughout the class, accommodations are being made for both high-achieving students as well as low-achieving students. The low-achieving students feel little pressure to "keep up" with the learning happening with the high-achieving students and the high-achieving students do not have to wait or slow down for the rest of the class. While an end date is set for students to complete the unit, this date is fluid and can often change if more or less time is needed as students progress. When students are ready to assess, they have the choice when they want to assess. There are often quite a few students who finish the unit before the set end date.

Oftentimes in a typical math classroom, one lesson is taught each day. It is the one-lesson-per-day mentality that most of us experienced as students ourselves. One lesson would be taught for the day, homework would be assigned, and it would be completed at home. The next day you would learn another lesson. One of the most simple – yet seemingly quite difficult for many – changes we can make as teachers is to eliminate the one-lesson-per-day mentality. It is easy to actually make the change of not teaching one lesson per day, and yet it is very difficult because we often sabotage ourselves as teachers. We make excuses about why it will not work or that we won't be able to cover all of the material needed if this happens. But when we eliminate teaching one lesson per day, we give kids a chance to learn the material within the time needed. There is no rushing to finish the lesson by the end of class. If the lesson isn't finished, it can be continued the next day. There is no need to rush students through a lesson in order to complete it by the end of class. If a lesson takes two or three days to complete, then that should be okay. Allow the time needed to teach concepts rather than trying to fit the lesson into a certain block of time. In addition, if a lesson takes a little more than a day and it is finished part way through the next day, then use the class time to start another lesson or possibly an activity that leads into the next lesson.

> One of the most simple – yet seemingly quite difficult for many – changes we can make as teachers is to eliminate the one-lesson-per-day mentality.

Assessing

Assessments are often thought of as paper tests given to students at the end of a unit in math. While these types of assessments can be great tools to assess student learning, there are other tools that allow students choice in proving their understanding of content. With any good assessment, students should always know the standards or expectations prior to each unit. This allows students to gain knowledge on the topics taught and what will be asked of them at the end of the unit.

One of the easiest ways for students to prove mastery is to give them the standards for the unit and ask them to "prove mastery." This allows them ownership over how to prove their knowledge on the content. Expectations should always be given to students in the form of a rubric or other document so students can clearly identify how to meet the standards/expectations for the unit. Students must know what is expected in order to prove mastery. For example, a grade 7 math standard says, "Use facts about supplementary, complementary, vertical, and adjacent angles in a multi-step problem to write and solve simple equations for an unknown angle in a figure." If students are asked to prove mastery over this standard, they can prove mastery through any method they choose. Whether it be a presentation, examples, a movie, or any other method, students have the option and ownership to choose how they will prove mastery. Students can have a few days in class to work on this. It is important that students submit it often to the teacher so feedback can be provided. Once feedback is given, students can revise and resubmit. This should be an ongoing loop until both the student and teacher agree that they have proved mastery. This is a much more powerful and rigorous way to assess students.

Another way to assess students is by simply having a conversation with them. By taking a few minutes to sit with a kid and ask them to prove a concept with you, you can assess their ability to solve that problem. Formal assessments don't have to always be used to assess a student's progress. A teacher, for example, could ask a student to prove a concept to another child while s/he assesses their ability to create, solve, and explain a concept. The power of conversation, feedback, and application are wonderful ways that a student can be assessed.

Lastly, letting students reassess to prove understanding of content should be encouraged in today's math classroom. Reassessments need not be lengthy, time consuming, or formal, and can be done in a multitude of ways. Students can be given a different assessment that is catered to that individual student. There would be no need for the student to complete an entire new assessment; instead, assign a few examples with which they have struggled. For example, if a student struggled with proving the converse of the Pythagorean Theorem, the teacher could ask the child to prove this standard to them. Ask the student specifically to prove the converse of the Pythagorean Theorem and provide examples supporting their explanation. By having students do the work and then provide a verbal explanation, insight is gained on whether students have met the standard/expectation. By allowing reassessments, you put the focus on the learning. A child who progresses forward to new content with a lack of understanding of previous content is not benefitting him-/herself or the teacher.

> By allowing reassessments, you put the focus on the learning. A child who progresses forward to new content with a lack of understanding of previous content is not benefitting him-/herself or the teacher.

Homework

Homework is often a key element of a math classroom. To what capacity and how it is factored into a grade usually depends on the teacher or group of teachers. For many years, I was consumed with grading homework. I was also a huge proponent of homework, but it always was a struggle for me to get students to complete it with fidelity. Once collected, it was a major burden to get it all scored and entered in a timely matter. Then the unthinkable happened. I stopped collecting and grading homework altogether. While homework was still assigned, it was now just practice and considered formative work. Rather than the focus being put on collecting and scoring homework, the focus was now placed on providing feedback on the formative work.

While on my third year of not collecting or grading formative work, students still complete this work when asked, as they see it is necessary for learning content. Previously, students did the work out of compliance. When homework was no longer graded, there was no motivation for students to quickly write down answers or cheat from others to complete the work. There was also no penalty for getting every answer incorrect. Oftentimes when students don't do the assigned work, it is because they don't understand it well enough and fear receiving a failing grade. When you take away the grade, students can get every problem incorrect without being penalized. Students can then use this knowledge, along with feedback from the teacher, to improve and correct their understanding of the content. As teachers, we can redirect our efforts into providing timely and accurate feedback to students during this formative process rather than collecting and grading formative work.

Teachers often struggle with the issue of homework completion. While many different methods to improve homework completion are tested, improvement is rarely made because the focus of homework completion is compliance, not learning. Once focus is put on the learning, rather than compliance, the focus of how you view homework changes.

The purpose of homework is to give extra practice to students in the form of formative work. Formative work, however, does not have to be given as homework. There are numerous ways that practice can be given to students without assigning work to be done at home. In-class activities, which include discovery activities, are key for student engagement. When introducing concepts, provide students with opportunities to learn on their own and to form their own ideas on the concept(s). For example, if students are learning about slope-intercept form, rather than teaching what $y = mx + b$ means, have students take the equation and practice graphing it however they choose to develop their own thoughts on what the m and b do to the equation. Students could also use graphing software to graph different values for m and b to gain insight on how the equation works before any formal lesson is given. Even more powerful would be to have students work in groups to bounce ideas off each other. At the end of the activity, students could present their findings to the class. The class, as a whole, then can work together to come up with their final thoughts. Once the activity is complete and students make their final thoughts, a lesson by the teacher can be given. By introducing students to a concept through discovery, students will better understand how it works and how to explain the concept before the lesson is taught.

Activities

One of the most powerful things that math teachers can do is to allow students to discover concepts before they are formally taught. Math teachers often start teaching a concept about which students are unfamiliar without allowing any opportunity for engagement with the concepts. By allowing students to play around with the concept, they are being allowed to interact with the concept. Even if they don't understand it completely, they are gaining knowledge that will help them make connections when the teacher explains the concepts.

For example, if students are beginning to learn about transformations of functions, they could be given a list of multiple functions they have never seen before (quadratic, exponential, etc.) and ask them to answer one question: "How do the letters a, b, h, and k affect an equation?" Students could be given the parent functions to all equations, each with a, b, h, and k. Allow students to plug in values for these variables and graph the results to make conclusions using a graphing calculator or software. For a day or more, students could be investigating these concepts while the teacher walks around asking questions while pushing them to investigate further. At the end of the activity, which may take multiple days, students can present their findings and as a class they can come up with a final answer to the original prompt. Once complete, the teacher can start the formal lesson. Students have gained insight to the concept through discovery and have a solid understanding of what this concept is prior to the teacher teaching the lesson. This not only helps students better understand concepts, but it gives them a chance to collaborate with others, make conclusions, and take ownership of what they are learning.

Student Choice/Ownership

Learning happens every day in a math classroom. What better way to improve student achievement than to allow student choice in all aspects of their learning? The students are the ones who are learning; therefore, they should have a stake in their own learning. Student choice can be applied to many different aspects of a classroom. From the physical set-up of a classroom to assessments, student choice can improve achievement. When giving students choice in the classroom, start small. By slowly implementing student choice, you can test certain techniques or practices to see if it works within your own classroom. Change takes time; allow time to implement this change.

The physical environment should be one in which students make the space their own in order to optimize achievement. While this may sometimes require a seating chart, allowing students to sit where they choose provides students the opportunity to collaborate with others. It is intimidating to give students freedom in the physical classroom environment but, with clear expectations, you can develop a collaborative and respectful environment for students. If your classroom environment allows, let students move their desks or tables as well. Students will often not only choose who they want to work with, but also where they want to sit. Some students may choose to sit on the floor or some may choose to stand. Allowing flexibility regarding where they sit provides students an opportunity to learn in a space most comfortable for them. If the space that the student chose is not working best for them, encourage them to find a space that is best for their learning rather than telling them they can't work where they have chosen. Often it takes only a few reminders for a student to find the best space for them to learn.

Student choice can also be provided during assessments. In a traditional math classroom, every student takes the test at the same time. By allowing students to take the assessments when they are ready, you are giving them the opportunity to be better prepared for an assessment. The date for the class assessment can still be given but allowing students some flexibility in choosing when they are ready to assess will provide for better results in student learning. Many students may work faster than the pace of the class but they cannot move ahead with content if they are waiting to take the assessment the same day as everyone else. By allowing these students to take the assessment early, they can continue with the content in class without having to wait for everyone else.

When students become bored waiting for others they can often become discipline problems. In addition, by allowing students to take an extra day or two to take their assessment you are providing them a better chance at success. By giving students these extra few days, they will have some more time to prepare for the assessment. If a student is not prepared for a test by the date given, it does no good to the student or the teacher for the student to take the assessment. This may take some time getting used to, and also it may provide some challenges when assessing, but the payoff in better student achievement is worth it.

Another aspect of student choice is giving them options on what they want to practice in class. Through the flipped classroom, students are able to use the entire class period to work on what they choose. Students can use their class period to work on practice, activities, or to watch videos of the content. They can plan ahead and use the class time as needed to learn. In one class period, multiple groups of students may be working on different areas within the unit. This allows students the choice to work on what they choose in class and take charge of their own learning. Students are not held back by the pace of the class and students who work slower don't have to speed through concepts if they need extra practice. By teaching students this model (and the expectations for it), an environment of collaboration and self-pacing can become the norm.

In the flipped classroom, students are allowed multiple ways to take ownership over what they are learning. One way that students can show understanding of concepts is by starting the class. This not only gives students another way to review instruction, but also provides the teacher with a snapshot of whether they understand the concept(s). A student is chosen a random to go to the board and the student starts explaining the concepts taught. This student explains as much as they want and then calls on another student. Students question each other, make their own examples, and fix each other's errors. The teacher doesn't intervene at all. As students explain their way through the concepts, the teacher gains insight into what concepts the students fully understand or which concepts students are struggling to understand.

While this process can be used in a flipped classroom, it could be adapted to any classroom where students explain concepts previously taught. At any point, a student could be called upon to go to the board and explain a concept. It is a model that must first be taught at the beginning of the school year. Once students practice this method and learn the expectations, it becomes a part of class that provides both students and the teacher with formative assessments to guide instruction for the class or the need for more practice. Students leading class allows them to take ownership of their learning to show understanding. It is a powerful way to hand over ownership to students.

Collaboration

Students must be allowed to work collaboratively every day in a math classroom. Collaboration provides students with the ability to verbalize their mathematical processing to others. This not only strengthens the student's understanding, but also helps other students who may not have not solved the math in that way. In math, there are multiple ways to learn most concepts. By allowing students to work together, you are giving them a platform to learn the different ways from each other.

For example, if students are learning about systems of equations, one student may solve the system of equations by substitution while another may use elimination. The teacher can facilitate learning by encouraging them to explain why they chose the methods they used. In addition, if one of the students incorrectly solved the problem, they can work together to get the correct solution. The power of collaboration gives students the voice to explain their mathematical thinking.

> Collaboration is not just about working together to get the correct answer. Collaboration can also mean creating something that proves understanding of a concept.

However, collaboration is not just about working together to get the correct answer. Collaboration can also mean creating something that proves understanding of a concept. Geometry students could be paired up to create a geometric proof that meets certain criteria. Students could work together to create a proof that, for example, uses triangle similarity. Within that proof, students can also use a multitude of other theorems, definitions, or postulates to prove understanding. Students work together to create an end result. This end result can be used as a formative assessment to guide instruction. Students may be asked to present their results to the rest of the class or possibly to parents.

I often use rope when students are learning about any aspect of graphing, which could include graphing linear equations or transformations. Using masking tape, groups of students create a coordinate grid on the floor. If students are learning about graphing linear equations, I may ask each group to create an equation that has a slope of -3 and a y-intercept of 7. Once they successfully use themselves as points and rope to represent the line, they are then asked to create a line perpendicular to that. During this entire process, students are asked to explain how they know or what they did to determine the answer. Not only are students working collaboratively to create an end result, but they are also verbalizing their understanding of the concepts. It also lets the teacher know which students may need more practice because they are struggling with content. Think of different ways you can use your spaces in the school to help you interact with mathematical concepts.

Letting Go

Speaking from personal experience, it is sometimes difficult to let go of what you have always done. As teachers, we can become set in our ways and it can be quite challenging to accept change within our own classroom. I was my biggest obstacle to changing what learning looked like in my own classroom. I liked having all of my students quiet, facing forward, and in rows. This was how my classroom had looked for over a decade. Whenever I was presented with a new idea or new way to try something, I was the one who told myself it wouldn't work in my classroom. It was very easy to make excuses for my own classroom. Let

> You are your biggest obstacle. By keeping an open mind and being open to change, you can transform your classroom to better serve your students.

go of what you have done in your classroom and revisit every aspect of how you teach if you are looking for significant and positive change. You are your biggest obstacle. By keeping an open mind and being open to change, you can transform your classroom to better serve your students.

Let go of everything that is known to be true in your classroom and rethink all aspects of what you do. Think about the outcomes you want and where your problem areas are. Where do you want to start? Start small and be persistent and open with your changes. Be honest with the students and let them know what you are doing but, more importantly, let them know why. Give them a voice in this process, allowing them to make suggestions for changes. Provide them a way to give feedback, both good and bad. This not only allows students to take ownership in their own class but it opens the dialogue between student and teacher to further build relationships.

Looking forward, put learning at the forefront of every decision you make. Think of something in your class that you want to change and the outcome that you desire. By focusing on the learning, add in student ownership and choice by trusting your students to be leaders within your class. Modeling the change and expected outcomes to students are keys to success. By starting small, change will happen, and you will innovate your math classroom to meet the needs of your students. Give students a voice and let them lead the change.

Reference

Bergmann, J. and Sams, A. (2015). 5 New Videos About Flipped Learning From Bermgann & Sams. Accessed October 8, 2018: www.flippedclassroomworkshop.com/5-new-vidoes-about-flipped-learning-from-bergmann-sams/

7

Librarians: Champions of Innovation!

Shannon McClintock Miller

Picture this: You walk into a school and hear noise echoing down the hall. You can't help but walk toward it and see that it is coming from the library. When you peek inside you see a space filled with activity, creativity, collaboration, learning, reading, and noise. There are groups of students gathered around the library at tables, on the floor, and even halfway out the door in the hallway. There are students creating in the makerspace and recording in a tiny green tent. There are teachers collaborating around a tall cafeteria table and coffee. Right outside the library, there are two classes Skyping with the author of the book they just read and have even invited several other schools around the world to join in.

As you look around, it is easy to notice these things are not contained within the library alone. There is a LEGO wall in the elementary hallway and students running robots up and down the hall in a race using math problems. Along with lots and lots of books, students are checking out maker-kits from the library and bringing them home. There is something going on in every little space within the library, outside of the library, and throughout the building. But if you stick around long enough, you will see that most of this activity starts at the heart of the school, which is the library.

You can't help but smile and wish this environment and these experiences on every single student, teacher, and community in schools everywhere. Not only is this library humming with activity, it is a place in which innovative practices pop up continuously throughout the year, largely because of the person at the center of this space. That person is the librarian.

Being a teacher librarian myself, I have embraced the change we can create within our library and school community through innovation. I oftentimes think about what innovation means to me, personally and as a librarian. As defined by the Merriam-Webster dictionary:

> Innovation, for its part, can refer to something new or to a change made to an existing product, idea, or field.

For in the library, we justify, tackle, and champion change every single day. And to serve as champions and leaders, we must take a step back and truly think about how we, as librarians, or as teachers, administrators, and even families, can support and cultivate the innovation that takes place with the librarian in the library and throughout the school community in person, online, and even globally.

You might be asking: What exactly does a librarian do that is so innovative? What does innovation look like in a library? How does the innovation put into play by the librarian effect all the members of the community?

Librarians can be the biggest champions and leaders for innovation within our communities because of the unique role and location we have in our buildings. We work with all of the students, teachers, administrators, and families, which enables us to touch the lives of each and every one with our unique and special innovative ideas, events, programs, spaces, and so much more. In this chapter I am going to share five ways librarians can be true champions and leaders of innovation. I will provide you with lots of practical strategies for becoming champions and leaders of innovation within your library, school community, and throughout the world too.

Even if you are not a librarian, remember that every single person in the building must work together to create the very best schools and experiences we can for our students and, ultimately, for the future of education. These partnerships are essential as we create something new and bring change to our schools. Our students need teacher librarians to help become lifelong readers and learners, and for their overall well-being, and all of our teacher librarians need you to support them and the importance of their roles as leaders and champions of innovation.

Relationships with All Stakeholders

One of the most important actions to undertake when leading innovation and creating a change within a library and community is to build and cultivate relationships with all of the stakeholders involved. The library needs to be the heart of the school and the place where these relationships not only start, but where they are grown and fostered every single day. Good relationships are the very first "why" and "how" of successful library programs and are found in libraries that show innovation.

> The library needs to be the heart of the school and the place where relationships not only start, but where they are grown and fostered every single day.

When I started my job at Van Meter Community School in Van Meter, Iowa, as the district teacher librarian, I was a member of the community, a mom of three young children, a volunteer in the library and my children's classrooms, and I served on the district technology committee. I was very involved in the PTA (Parent–Teacher Association) and volunteered for everything under the sun. I was also a substitute teacher and even did a long-term substitute teaching job for the teacher librarian who was there before me when she was on maternity leave. I had one foot in the door when I started at Van Meter because of the relationships I had with everyone at school, including the students, and within our community.

However, as the year started, I soon realized the relationships I would build within our school community were not only tied to the personal relationships with important people. The relationships were also tied to the physical space of the library and the way people felt when they came to our space. I had to build and cultivate these relationships even more because I wanted people to associate them with what could and would happen within the library and throughout the building with me as the librarian and with our library as the heart of the school. Because of the way I built relationships and trust, our library program changed and became the library program we wanted it to be. With relationships at the center of our library, we had one of the most innovative library programs within the state and country. We were making a difference regarding how libraries were perceived and how they had been in the past.

When you start building relationships, it is important to think about what these relationships will mean to you and the library program. Ask yourself questions like: What can the community do to add to our library program? How can the community help with changing things in the library? What new concepts and ideas can the community bring to the table? How can I be there for everybody involved when we are creating this change?

Since these relationships include everyone within the community, it is also important to think about where the different groups are at so we can connect with them in effective and meaningful ways. We can make our library welcoming so we can get students through the door. We can show up in classrooms to collaborate and co-teach. We can have a substantial presence in the professional development of our school, which helps us build capacity and trust with teachers. We can kick off the year and other family school events with a bang as we WOW families with how we are an integral part of the school system and, again, how the library can be the heart of the school.

We can also use social media tools to build community. We can create a Facebook page or group, or a Twitter, Instagram, Snapchat, or Pinterest account, and other such tools to build community for our library. This is one of the best things I did for our library as I connected with everyone and showcased what was happening within our library and school throughout the school year. In addition, we can use these social networks to connect and build relationships with others around the world, which will ultimately affect our students and teachers as we make these connections and find ways to not only build relationships but to collaborate and connect in meaningful ways too.

I also love using Skype and Google Hangouts for building relationships with others. These can be organized with libraries and students a few miles away or halfway around the world. With these digital tools, connecting has never been easier or more impactful on our communities. By using Skype and Google Hangouts, I was able to build relationships with other schools, libraries, librarians, teachers, students, authors, illustrators, experts, zoos, farms, and the list goes on and on. The ways and places you can connect using Skype and Google Hangouts are endless.

And of course, don't forget the relationships you can build with your administrators. These are some of the most important of all when implementing and championing innovation within the library and as you have an impact on the entire school. If you want to lead innovation within your school, don't ask to be invited. Show up and get a seat at the table, because others will soon realize that your voice matters to your students, families, teachers, and most of all, to them as they inspire to lead innovation with your help and talents.

> If you want to lead innovation within your school, don't ask to be invited. Show up and get a seat at the table, because others will soon realize that your voice matters.

The relationships you have with the public library and librarian are also very important. As you begin to start something new and implement changes, unique ways you can collaborate with the public library will pop up and can be carried out even more than ever before. You will find value in this relationship and the resources and ways it can support your work in the school library. You can also have an impact on the public library and the innovation happening there.

Physical and Online Spaces

We hear a lot lately about library and school spaces. They look and sound different than they have in the past, with lots of flexible and comfortable seating, technology, movable shelving, creative shapes including shelves and furniture, natural and synthetic lights, makerspaces, and welcoming entrances that encourage and support active learning, exciting noise, creativity, reading, connecting, and more. These are spaces which live and breathe innovation.

Libraries need to be designed to support inquiry and collaboration of all kinds, becoming a place which serves as the heart of the school. The library space needs to constantly support the learning of students, teachers, and even families. It needs to change with the times as new products, ideas, and teaching methods come into play. It needs to accommodate personalized learning, project-based learning, and any learning methods and ideas that students and teachers want to try out and implement.

As librarians, we can be leaders within the library and other spaces within our building and community by embracing all changes and supporting all types of spaces. We need to research, visit, and try out different ideas for learning spaces while curating these for our community. It is also important to include students while doing this research and making decisions. After all, it is the space they will take on as their own as they learn, connect, read, create, and collaborate with one another.

The spaces we create online for our libraries are also essential. These need to be open 24/7; somewhere our students can once again be connected to so many different learning and reading resources, creative experiences, collaborative relationships, and special events. As reading and learning becomes more and more interactive, our digital spaces will become more and more important and a way for everyone to have amazing learning experiences at school, home, and on the go. If our schools can implement that type of space, we can feel confident they will support the anytime learning our students need.

Just as we cultivate relationships by meeting our patrons where they are, we need to create spaces where they want to come. As Kevin Costner's character hears while walking through the field in *Field of Dreams* (1989), "If you build it, they will come."

Collaboration

According to the Merriam-Webster dictionary,

> Collaboration is the action of working with someone to produce or create something.

With innovation referring to "something new or to a change made to an existing product, idea, or field," you can see why collaboration is essential for an innovative library and school culture.

Collaboration goes hand in hand with our library spaces and with the relationships we build and foster within them. While these elements develop and grow, collaboration can happen in an authentic, meaningful, and very productive way. To be successful, collaboration needs to be constant, consistent, flexible, and built on relationships and trust. By being flexible and ever-changing, we know that collaboration will fit into the innovation that is taking place with our students, teachers, community, and others around the world.

> To be successful, collaboration needs to be constant, consistent, flexible, and built on relationships and trust.

About two years into my job as the teacher librarian at Van Meter, I was collaborating on a consistent basis with about half of the K–12 teachers. It wasn't that I didn't want to or didn't have the time to collaborate with the other half; it was just more challenging to collaborate with some. It could have been I didn't know their curriculum or what was happening in their classroom, or perhaps I didn't feel confident. It could have been that we just didn't find the time or even make time to collaborate. Or perhaps it was just the fact that we didn't connect or feel like we had important things to talk about. But this wasn't good enough for me. If I was going to make the impact I knew I could and support the school like I should, I needed to step up my game as a leader and collaborator within our school district.

So I took a step back and created a space where we could build relationships, sharing and creating plans in order to implement a successful program of collaboration across the school into each and every classroom, and with every teacher and myself. This Google Doc (see Figure 7.1) would not only be a place for amazing and meaningful collaboration to take place, it would be a place for others to see what was happening in the academic classrooms, library, and the related arts classes, too.

With this Google Doc, I knew exactly what was happening in a classroom on a monthly basis and could collaborate, plan, and create amazing learning experiences with the teachers for our students better than ever before. Our administrators also appreciated that they could now see the collaboration that was taking place between us. The teachers would add what was happening within their classrooms and curriculum. They would

FIGURE 7.1

add resources, books, websites, links, and whatever extra information was needed. I would then go into the Google Doc and add ideas, books, resources, links, digital tools and apps, and most all of a plan for how we could work together to create the best experiences for our students.

When I met with the teachers, we would use this Google Doc to guide our conversations about what we were working on and what was coming up. We also used it as a place to document those quick conversations that happened in the hallway, library, or even in emails or texts. It kept us all on the same page and made those precious moments together, both in person and virtually, really count.

I collaborated with all teachers, including all the special education, "Talented and Gifted," reading specialists, physical education, and other related arts teachers. One of the best parts of having all of us together in the same Google Doc was the collaboration that also happened across grade levels and specialties. For example, maybe the grade 1 students were getting ready to videotape their community projects they had been working on in the classroom, art room, and library. At the same time, our grade 4 students are learning more of the editing features in iMovie. We could partner them up for one of the class periods for some great peer-to-peer teaching. It was a win–win for everyone. We all loved it when collaborations like this took place.

As you think about collaboration and ideas such as this one, think about how the collaborative partnerships you establish will support the innovation within your library and school community. How will collaboration support what you want to do that is innovative? How is collaboration supporting and pushing the teachers within their innovative ideas and methods of teaching? How is collaboration creating the culture and space you want to have as the core of your library program? And most importantly: Is the collaboration supporting all of your students in ways that will help them be successful? Here are a few tips to help you as you begin collaborating with your colleagues and others:

♦ Always say yes to your colleagues and find a way to help with anything needed. Together you will find solutions and wonderful ways to work together.

♦ Don't wait to be invited to collaborate. Show up. WOW your colleagues with what you know and can do to help. Be their best support. Figure out their favorite treat or drink. Be creative about how you meet if you can't find time during the school day. My second superintendent, John Carver, and I used to meet for coffee on Saturdays, when I helped him with social media and blogging. Now that collaboration definitely made a difference!

♦ Have fun collaborating! It is always one of the most rewarding parts of our jobs, and the students and families appreciate this effort and benefit from these relationships too.

And don't forget, collaboration doesn't have to happen with just the teachers within your building and district. Collaboration happens with your students, teachers, and others that you meet within your state, country, and globally. Some of my best moments of collaboration have been with friends and colleagues halfway around the world.

You can read "My Tips & Helpful Google Docs For Awesome Collaboration Between Teacher Librarians and Teachers," on my blog, The Library Voice, here: http://vanmeterlibraryvoice. blogspot.com/2018/07/tips-for-awesome-collaboration-between.html

Literacy

As the K–12 teacher librarian in our school district, I support and inspire all of our readers: students, teachers, and families alike. I am constantly looking for ways to not only champion and support a special culture of reading within our community, but also striving to develop a wonderfully diverse and rich library collection and culture of reading.

Within the "Future Ready Librarians" framework (see Figure 7.2), *Literacy* is one of the most important parts of each one of the eight wedges. Literacy is found around the middle circle of *Learner Centered* and focuses not only on all learners

FIGURE 7.2

and readers, but throughout the entire framework including *Cultivates Community Partnerships*, *Designs Collaborative Spaces*, *Empowers Students as Creators*, and more.

As defined within the framework, as Future Ready Librarians we:

> *inspire and support the reading lives of both students and teachers while creating inclusive collections that acknowledge and cele-brate diverse experiences and provide instructional opportunities to empower learners as effective users and creators of information and ideas.*

As librarians, we need to be the ones who champion and lead a culture of innovative literacy practices within our library and community. Not only can we promote reading within our schools and community, we can now connect with others around the world in literacy events such as "World Read Aloud Day" and "Dot Day." We can include authors, illustrators, publishers, and others in discussions with our students through tools like Skype, and connect with them through Twitter, Instagram, and Snapchat. These literary and artist heroes not only connect with our reading community; they become teachers, mentors, and, oftentimes, friends.

As readers, we are no longer bound to what is on the shelf, as we have options including eBooks, databases, audio books, and interactive reading experiences that hook even the most reluctant readers. The way we interact with literacy is changing through reading experiences that include virtual and augmented reality such as 4D from Capstone Publishing, and Spy Quest, videos, choose your own virtual reading adventure, interactive eBooks such as Lightbox from Follett, and much more. As we bring reading to life for readers, we are capturing their attention and harnessing their imagination.

Excitingly, we now have the innovative resources to let all of our readers bring their reading to life through interactive, digital storytelling tools and apps. As they read and share a favorite picture or chapter book, students can then hop onto digital storytelling tools such as Buncee or Storybird to create their own digital story. They can publish these digitally and share them with classmates, family members, and others throughout the world. To see their ideas brought to life and to be given a platform to tell stories is one more way we, as librarians and educators, can champion readers imaginations, ideas, and needs. Won't it be fun to see where reading will take our students next?

Technology

When I was getting my Masters in Library Science from the University of Northern Iowa 12 years ago, Van Meter

Community School was implementing its very first 1:1 laptop program within our district. I served on the District Technology Committee as a parent and then as the teacher librarian. As we went into this 1:1 journey, I decided to focus my thesis work on this topic too. Not only did I see the importance of a 1:1 program for our students and teachers, but I soon realized the leadership opportunities and change it would offer me as the teacher librarian at Van Meter.

It was so much more than just putting laptops into the hands of the students. By integrating technology into the classroom, library, homes of our families, and throughout the community, we were giving our students a voice and ways to showcase their creativity, knowledge, and passions. We were empowering them to be creative, connected, collaborative, and most of all innovative within their education and in all areas of their lives. This huge shift in our school community brought wonderful opportunities to the innovative culture and educational experiences we were creating for our students while connecting them to the world. From my perspective as the teacher librarian, the change it brought was hands-down one of the best things that ever could have happened to the teachers, library program, school community, and, of course, the Van Meter students.

As we slowly integrated technology throughout the school community, we added more and more digital tools and apps focusing on digital storytelling, gaming, virtual and augmented reality, coding, graphic design, robotics, and so much more. With this shift in resources and services, it meant that my expertise and innovative nature was needed more and more. I soon became the one that was integrating technology throughout the school and within classrooms through teachers and instruction. I became the local resident technology expert and loved the excitement this task brought. I had definitely found my niche and the success that accompanied it.

It became a passion of mine to learn about all the different resources and assist in the integration of these tools and the technology within the classrooms. Collaboration became more important than ever! As already mentioned earlier, with innovation referring to "something new or to a change made to an existing product, idea, or field," you can see why collaboration is essential for an innovative library and school culture. This couldn't be more true with the integration of technology throughout our school community.

Through collaborative work with the teachers and students, I found many opportunities to take this collaboration outside of the four walls of our school to the developers, publishers, and pioneers of this new and developing technology. I was driven to learn as much as I could and to be more effective in the implementation. Not only did I develop relationships with the pioneers, my students and teachers did too. When we learned about a new digital tool or app, I reached out to have them Skype with my community and learn from the ones who were the creators and developers. When we had questions or problems, we used Twitter to ask questions and find solutions. When our students had something amazing to show, they used social media and other avenues to show the world. These connections empowered them to ask questions, to problem solve, and to act as testers, mentors, and friends to the larger world of technology.

One of the best examples of this communication was when we Skyped with Allen Murray, one of the original creators of Halo. After a small group of high school students challenged me to connect with the creator of Halo, I jumped on Twitter and sent out a tweet. We were all surprised when Allen actually reached out and offered to Skype with the teens to answer questions, give them the inside scoop on the development of this popular game, and to play Halo with them in the library. Can you imagine the surprise of the students when I announced over the intercom one day, "Hey students. Feel free to come to the library to Skype and play with the creator of Halo, Allen Murray." It not only comprised something meaningful and important from the technology in their lives, it was a way for me to show them the power of technology, and it harnessed their passions for gaming, programming, and technology overall. It opened the doors for many students as they realized these passions could be turned into an amazing lifelong career.

Most all of, technology empowered our students to become lifelong learners, creators, and collaborators empowered to change the world through so many opportunities for innovation in the digital world we are all part of. After all, technology is one of the keys we can use to empower students as they become life learners and the ones who will bring change to education and to the future of our world. When technology is used in meaningful ways, it can be a vehicle to celebrate the differences, passions, and uniqueness of each and every student within our libraries and schools.

> When technology is used in meaningful ways, it can be a vehicle to celebrate the differences, passions, and uniqueness of each and every student within our libraries and schools.

Final Reflections

I would like to leave you with one of my favorite quotes that makes me think about innovation within education, especially as related to our school libraries and students:

> The first step in teaching students to innovate is making sure that educators have opportunities to be innovators themselves.
>
> Boss (2012)

I challenge you to think about this quote as you think about being an innovative librarian and educator while empowering those within your library, school, and community to be innovative too.

Innovation is about everyone. It is constant, always changing, and supports the wildest ideas, most far-out dreams, and extreme change like we can only imagine. As librarians and educators, we should never settle for the status quo or think innovation is something that stops or stands still just because we aren't "the students" in our libraries or classrooms. In fact, we all need to be the students as we embrace innovation, along with those wildest ideas, most far-out dreams, and the extreme change that we can make happen by partnering with everyone who makes up our community to *make* change happen.

Get ready, friends. We have a lot to look forward to as we embrace an innovative spirit and encourage others to do the same. After all, innovation should be the driver when thinking about what we should be doing to create the best experiences for our students today and in the future. We, as librarians, are definitely the champions and leaders of innovation that our students, communities, and the world needs!

Reference

Boss, S. (2012). *Brining Innovation to School: Empowering Students to Thrive in a Changing World*. Bloomington, IN: Solution Tree Press.

8

Sparking Innovation from Failure

Katrina Keene

Often, in our successes, we attribute our accomplishments to a positive role model in our lives. Graduation speeches, weddings, keynotes, and a new job can often spark memories of a person who helped shape us to be who we are. My story, however, is quite the opposite. In fact, the person who took away my spark, energy, confidence, and happiness for teaching is the one whom I thank today.

Early in my teaching career, I thought of myself as a "cutting edge" educator. I felt quite innovative, as I brought video conferencing into my classroom nearly 20 years ago. Sharing my love, knowledge, and expertise of technology with my students brought me great pleasure. I thrived on their smiles and excitement when my little kindergarten "technologists" asked for more time on the computer or ran home to tell mom and dad what they created or designed that day. I felt invincible as I changed the lives of students through the use of technology and strived to learn more by completing my Masters in Instructional Technology.

Upon finishing my degree, I moved into a few different positions, one being a technology coach. After three years of working with teachers, I found that I missed the students and the excitement that teaching brought to my life. I returned to the classroom by taking a grade 1 teaching position within a new district.

At the end of summer I arrived at my new classroom to set up. I couldn't wait to bring my new technological "experiences" to my students. As I looked around the classroom, I noticed old desks, broken chairs, and one table for guided reading. I searched and searched through cabinets and in every corner for computers, but there were none to be found. Being that I was new, I went to my grade 1 team leader to ask where I could "pick up" my computers. She informed me that we did not have computers as they were not needed to teach with. As a perceived innovator, I was saddened by this news but knew I had to fix the problem that was placed before me. According to Roth (2012):

> Innovators are the people who do things, not those who think about what could be done.

I searched online garage sales to find computers as well as new tables for my students. I came across four old iMacs as well as six round tables and picked them up from the man who was selling them. I loaded them all in my van and couldn't wait to get back to my school to set them up. I was on my way to creating the innovative classroom I had pictured when I took the job just a few months prior.

The Steps to My Innovative Classroom

According to Naz and Murad (2017), "The focus of innovative teaching is based on the trust that every student has the capacity to learn and be successful in life." The authors go on to say:

> A teacher should perceive each student as possessing unique personality characteristics that can be more polished by using creative and innovative teaching methods.
>
> Naz and Murad (2017, p.2)

> Educators often ask me how they can be more innovative in the classroom. Their minds race to technology as the only form of innovation; however, innovative teachers provide various ways for students to express their creativity and ideas.

Educators often ask me how they can be more innovative in the classroom. Their minds race to technology as the only form of innovation; however, innovative teachers provide various ways for students to express their creativity and ideas. I, too, chose to bring technology into each of my classrooms, but continually recognized that all students should have a voice in how they demonstrated their learning, aside from technology. Although my students always had other ways of providing evidence of their learning, technology always seemed to be the favorite and most popular choice for my students to "voice" their learnings and experiences in my classroom.

Considering Learning Spaces

I wasn't sure what to do with all the old desks that were in my classroom but I took a chance and pushed them into the hallway, making room for the new tables. I set up my students in groups so they could work collaboratively on projects. I could not fathom having my students in single desks as it felt old, tired, and extremely teacher centered. At the time I hadn't researched much on learning spaces or classroom design but I did know what made students thrive. Long (2018) believes, "The emphasis on learning means that we must also think about the learner." The author goes on to say:

> Learning spaces are not mere containers for a few, approved activities; instead, they provide *environments for people*. Factors such as the availability of food and drink, comfortable chairs, and furniture that supports a variety of learning activities are emerging as critical in the design of learning spaces – evidence of the second trend, giving consideration to human factors as integral to learning space design.
>
> Long (2018, p.1)

I used one of the six tables as a computer station and also put one of the four computers on my guided reading table. I wanted to work with my students and guide them through the use of technology as they had never been exposed to it in kindergarten.

Being that it was the beginning of the year, I wanted my grade 1 students to tell me more about themselves. I loaded Kidspiration, a "cross-curricular visual workspace for K-5 learners," on each of the four new computers that I had purchased, and asked my students to build a web about who they were as a person (Inspiration Software, 2018). According to Naz and Murad, "A significant part of valuing students and facilitating their success lies in knowing them" (2017, p.2). But not only did this activity tell me more about each of my students, I was also able to evaluate their knowledge of letters, letter sounds, sentence structure, and even personality. We had a blast with this task, using the guided reading table to begin their webs then moving over to the computer station to complete them. Once their webs were built, my students asked if we could print them and hang them in the hall for Open House night. They were proud, thrilled, and ready to take on new activities and challenges.

Adopting Technology Myself

Rogers' diffusion theory addresses how administrators and teachers perceive technology adoption and integration in schools (2003). Rogers offers suggestions for why certain technological innovations might or might not be adopted. He suggests that before a person adopts an innovation, he or she goes through five stages of decision making that inform the person's attitude about the innovation. Figure 8.1 summarizes the stages involved in the innovation–decision process. Rogers believes that adoption of an innovation occurs when "a decision is made to make full use of an innovation as the best course of action available" (2003, p.177).

Ever since I was young, I was always "in the know" about new technologies and was also curious about old ones. I remember playing with my dad's eight track and record player thinking they were amazing. I was astonished at CDs when they first came out and bought as many as I could through a mail order program. Looking back, I feel I was fortunate to have a computer at home as well as at school. Even back in 1985, my teachers took

	Stage	*Occurrence*
Step I	Knowledge	Adopters gain an understanding of how the innovation works
Step II	Persuasion	Adopters form an opinion about the innovation
Step III	Decision	Adopters participate in activities that lead to acceptance or rejection
Step IV	Implementation	The innovation is adopted and put to use
Step V	Confirmation	Adopters seek the opinion of another person(s) to confirm or reverse the decision of the adoption

FIGURE 8.1
Source: Rogers (2003)

the class to the computer lab to type stories and bind them into books. I still have all of my books to this day.

I owe my innovative nature to both of my parents as well as my teachers. I often pass through the five stages of adopting an innovation with ease, as new technologies and their implementation excite me. It never crossed my mind not to share new technologies with my students and I always challenge myself to find new ways to implement them in terms of curriculum, standards, and classroom space. Throughout the year that I taught grade 1 and bought computers for my students, it didn't occur to me that other educators, including my building administrator, didn't adopt technologies and innovations the way that I did. I assumed all educators wanted technology in their classrooms and researched ways to integrate it.

Overcoming Lack of Support

Two weeks after hanging the Kidspiration pictures in the hallway, I received a call on my classroom intercom. It was the principal's secretary asking me to report to the office for a meeting. When I arrived to the meeting, I was greeted by the entire grade 1 team, principal, vice principal, and reading specialist. What I didn't know was that the meeting was about me. I was questioned on the pictures that were hanging in the hallway and told that technology was "not something we do at this school." According to Sheppard and Brown (2014, p.85):

Technology has become a routine part of how school-age students live, socialize, play, work, and learn; however, it appears that most public school classrooms remain largely unchanged.

As I listened to my team and principal talk, all I could picture in my head were my students. They had worked so hard on their webs and were looking forward to more technology use that very next week. By the end of the meeting, I was instructed to remove the computers as well as the tables from my classroom and conduct my lessons in the "traditional way." I was devastated, lost, and also confused at what had just happened to me and my students.

According to Neben (2014, p.44):

All innovations are not equal when it comes to the rate at which members of the social system adopt their use; some innovations may be adopted over a period of years while others may take decades.

Adding web creation software to my classroom didn't seem innovative to me at the time. I had come from other schools where I was already video conferencing with my students before video conferencing was even introduced into the education world. Then I realized innovations are not always adopted at the same rate, especially in education. What seemed simple and obvious to me was not so simple and obvious for my team, nor my administration. Gillard and colleagues (2010) concluded that 3% of educators (known as *techies*) adopt a new technology immediately; 10% of educators (known as *visionaries*) tend to adopt technologies following the previous group; 35% of educators (known to be *receptive to technology*) will adopt next; and 35% of educators (known as *skeptics*) must be convinced to adopt the new technology. The final 17% of educators (known as *laggards*) oppose the technology and will not adopt it.

The rest of the school year proved to be difficult for me as I taught my students under the watchful eyes of my team and administration. They were careful to make sure I was not using technology nor bringing in any types of innovations that might change the way in which teachers were instructed to teach at this school. The leader of my team made me put the old desks in rows and "re-taught" me how to teach like her. I felt alone and often cried during lunch. I felt I had nowhere and no one to turn to for answers or even support.

Although the year was 2009, I was slow to use Twitter and social media in ways that could have been beneficial to my mental and professional well-being. Looking back I wish I had connected with other educators around the world to know that not including technology was detrimental to my students. According to Siew:

> When experiences, values, and norms are shared among the members of a social network, this enhances the diffusion of information and promotes adoption.
>
> Singh and Hardaker (2014, p.111)

I questioned everything I knew about teaching, all the way down to if I was meant to be an educator at all. At the end of the school year I decided not to return to the school and also made the decision to leave teaching completely. I took a job as an Executive Director at a nearby private early childhood center where I learned everything about running a business as well as what it meant to be an administrator. About a year into the job it hit me that I wanted to study more about innovation and learn how to better support the teachers in my center. I began my Doctorate in Education and focused on technology integration and the rate at which innovations are adopted in education:

> Innovation is to be regarded as an instrument of necessary and positive change.
>
> Serdyukov (2017, p.5)

Finding Connections and Inspiration beyond One's School

After completing my Doctorate I began to wonder what happened to the teachers and administration at my school. I found out 14 teachers had left the same year that I did and that the principal had been demoted to an assistant principal at another school. Thinking about those 14 teachers led me to ponder the assumption that if I had been more connected via social media to those teachers, as well as to others outside of my school, perhaps I would have been better equipped to know how to deal with a school that resisted technology and innovation.

I reflected on my administration and finally began the journey to finding answers to what happened to me years prior. I was hurting for my administrator as I now knew I should have worked with her to bring new technologies into my classroom and the whole school. Even if I informed her and she still resisted, perhaps I could have found a way to train her or work together to ultimately benefit all students. According to Mingaine (2013, p.32):

> A positive attitude of school leader towards implementation of technology will encourage the school community to be actively involved in its implementation.

Feeling motivated to use my new knowledge and understanding about the adoptions of innovation, I applied for a position within a K–12 school. I went to the interview starry-eyed and ready to take on the world. I was offered the position and began my journey as their new Director of Technology.

Getting Others on Board

Throughout my role as Director of Technology, I went to Twitter and leaned on my Personal Learning Network (PLN) for advice on integration, adopting new technologies, and overall research on which technologies would work best for my school. Connecting myself was the best decision I ever made in my 18 years as an educator. I was now armed and ready for those teachers who were not ready to adopt something new. I focused my efforts on professional development and the training of what innovation is and how it can be brought into education. I quickly determined that slower and more targeted training was key to the success of the adoption of innovations in education.

It was 2012 and I was already challenging the teachers and administrators with augmented reality (AR), virtual reality (VR), video conferencing, robotics, and coding. It was important to me to build opportunities for creation, rather than consumption, as I wanted the students to deliver products. At the time, there were not many resources on AR and VR so I had to get innovative with their application in the classroom. Rolling out a K–12 AR program was both fun and frustrating as few teachers grasped on to the new technology.

My office was located in the media center and I often watched students as they returned their books. With every book that was returned, I wondered what they thought of the book and/or if it made a difference in their education. I couldn't help but want to create some type of system to know what students thought of the books they were reading. The program or system I ultimately created consisted of a full media center AR integration as both teachers and students created "book talks" on each book they read. According to Niemann and Wolpers (2010):

> Augmented Reality (AR) is a term describing those technologies that allow the real-time mixture between computer-generated digital content and the real world.

In addition, Agogi adds (2011, p.16):

> AR can also be defined as being an overlay or superimposing of digital data visualised on top of the real view of the surrounding environment.

Once the AR video target was tagged to the book, everyone, including parents, had the ability to enjoy a short synopsis just by scanning the book with the AR app. A few teachers ran with the new technology and began making educational scavenger hunts around the school. Other teachers shied away from the technology. One grade 2 teacher loved this new way of learning so much that she started overlaying student-created targets (or videos) on top of various artworks that her students created. She tried to bring her team on board but was disappointed when their excitement didn't match her own. It took me back to my experience as a grade 1 teacher, challenged with the disappointing looks I received from my students when they entered the "computer-less classroom" after my administrator took them away. I looked at the grade 2 teacher, recognizing her pain and confusion about why her team wouldn't jump on board with the new exciting opportunities, and it hit me. Just like that, an image of my administrator popped into my head and all I could think about was wanting to find her and thank her.

Helping Others through the Adoption Stages

I spent years searching for an answer to why things happened the way they did at my old school. But now I had my answer. I was able to explain to the grade 2 teacher that her team just wasn't ready to adopt a new technology. I told her about the stages a person goes through and explained what had happened to me.

What if my administrator was slower to adopt an innovation? What if it scared her? Knowing that only 3% of educators adopt a new technology immediately, and 17% of educators will never adopt it, perhaps my administrator was in the middle 80% of educators who had to be convinced? This realization allowed me to challenge fellow educators to work with their teams with the acceptance that others may be slower to adopt. This revelation was like a switch in my life. I had a renewed sense of education as a whole and knew that my calling was to challenge educators to adopt innovations in a non-threatening and fun way.

Five years later, I moved from being a Director of Technology to working for a Fortune 500 company where I helped schools redesign their classrooms to accommodate innovative teaching. It proved interesting, as everything I had done almost 20 years ago for my students was found in the most recent research to be "favorable for student learning." Most recently, I began running my own business as well as working with an EdTech start-up to help schools and educators bring computer science into their classrooms. Being able to work with educators and administrators is an extreme honor for me as I once thought I was done with the education profession. Through years of research on innovation, I learned something that I never knew would come out of a Doctoral degree program: Patience and understanding. Two qualities that seem so simple were ones I had to learn how to possess.

Education is constantly inundated with new innovations and I challenge both administrators and fellow educators to be patient with those who are slower to adopt. It is only a small percentage of us who race to the Apple store to buy the newly released iPhone and it's a small percentage of us who are equipped to understand why and how an educator doesn't jump on the next best innovation released. Perhaps we can learn a few things from those "skeptics and laggards." They could have a bigger plan in mind for their students and need more time to sort out the details. Whatever the case, be one who celebrates *all* educators. You are not a failure if someone whom you are trying to influence doesn't adopt a new trend. Keep your mind and heart open to all and know that your spark can be ignited even by someone who you'd never think possible.

References

Agogi, E. (2011). "Augmented reality in education." Proceedings: "Science Center To Go" Workshops. Athens, Greece.

Gillard, S., Bailey, D., and Nolan, E. (2010). "Ten reasons for IT educators to be early adopters of IT innovations." *Journal of Information Technology Education*, 7, 21–33.

Inspiration Software. (2018). Kidspiration. Accessed October 2, 2018: www.inspiration.com/Kidspiration

Long, P. (2018). Chapter 9: Trends in Learning Space Design. Accessed October 2, 2018: www.educause.edu/research-and-publications/books/learning-spaces/chapter-9-trends-learning-space-design

Mingaine, L. (2013). "Leadership challenges in the implementation of ICT in public secondary schools, Kenya." *Journal of Education and Learning*, 2(1), 32–43.

Naz, F. and Murad, H. (2017). "Innovative teaching has a positive impact on the performance of diverse students." *SAGE Open*, Oct–Dec, 1–8.

Neben, J. (2014). "Attributes and barriers impacting diffusion of online education at the institutional level: Considering faculty perceptions." *Distance Learning*, 11(1), 41–50.

Niemann, K. and Wolpers, M. (2010). "Real world object based access to architecture learning material – The mace experience." Proceedings: World Conference on Educational Multimedia, Hypermedia and Telecommunications (EDMEDIA 2010). Toronto, Canada.

Rogers, E. M. (2003). *Diffusion of Innovations,* 5th ed. New York: The Free Press.

Roth, Y. (2012, March 16). Is Theodore Levitt's Article "Creativity is not enough" Still Accurate Today? Accessed October 2, 2018: https://yannigroth.com/2012/03/16/is-theodore-levitts-article-creativity-is-not-enough-still-accurate-today/

Serdyukov, P. (2017). "Innovation in education: What works, what doesn't, and what to do about it?" *Journal of Research in Innovative Teaching and Learning*, 10(1), 4–33.

Sheppard, B. and Brown, J. (2014). "Leadership for a new vision of public school classrooms." *Journal of Educational Administration*, 52(1), 84–96.

Singh, G. and Hardaker, G. (2014). "Barriers and enablers to adoption and diffusion of Elearning: A systematic review of the literature – a need for an integrative approach." *Education and Training*, 56(2–3), 105–21.

9

Innovating Personal Skill Development

Dwight Carter

People are hired for job skill but are fired for personal skill. – Tim Kight, Focus 3

I recently completed my 24th year as an educator and it's been an amazing journey. I contribute much of my professional success to a number of mentors and school leaders. I've attended, participated in, and facilitated hundreds of professional learning opportunities to hone my craft as an educator, such as how to write effective lesson plans, differentiating instruction, understanding by design, integrating technology in the classroom, data analysis, and so on. However, the last two years, I've participated in what I consider to be the most impactful learning journey of my career: An intentional focus on personal skill development.

Great educators understand, embrace, and take responsibility for their own professional development. They participate or lead in book studies, Twitter chats, and webinars. They attend and/or present at local and national conferences, and they take time to reflect on their craft. All these things are a part of skill development. As we face a number of disruptions as 21st century educators, we need the type of professional learning that helps us respond appropriately to disruptions such as: more complex diversity issues, the growing need for transparency, a much more intense focus on student safety, and accelerated technology advancements to name a few. What comes with these disruptions is the need to understand the impact of our own behavior on a school's climate and culture.

> There are two things we have absolute control over: Our attitude and our actions.

There are two things we have absolute control over: Our attitude and our actions. In such disruptive, divisive, and polarizing times, we often forget about what we can actually control. There is so much finger pointing, blame gaming, and general disregard for others that it may feel like things are spiraling out control. I am reminded of the words that educator, author, and speaker George Couros often posits: "Make the positive so loud that the negative cannot be heard." This is, however, much easier said than done.

When I became a head principal in 2005, I used "Be Great" as my sign off on all correspondence. At first, it was a simple message to inspire others regardless of the content of the message in the letter or email. I actually thought it was a bit cheesy, so I stopped using it. A couple of staff members noticed the change and asked why I stopped using it. They said they enjoyed it and that it did, in fact, inspire them to think differently. I was shocked by their comments and continued to use it for the remainder of the school year. I still use it to this day and it has now become my mantra. A few years ago, I took some time to reflect on what it really means to me to "Be Great" and came up with the following acronym:

Be Grateful: Demonstrate an attitude of gratitude for my loving family, supportive network of friends and colleagues, and God's daily blessings, as well the "problemtunities" (opportunities disguised as problems) that come my way.

Be Relational: Focus on the people who have breathed life into me with words of encouragement, constructive criticism to help me grow, and remember that, "no significant learning occurs without significant relationships" (Dr. James Comer). I can improve relationships with others by being an active listener, reserving judgment, being present, and demonstrating empathy.

Be *Enthusiastic:* It is often said that, "nothing great was ever achieved without enthusiasm" (Ralph Waldo Emerson). I firmly believe this and have seen it happen in my life and in the lives of others. I try to begin each day enthused about the opportunity to positively change lives and impact the future of others, which is my personal mission statement!

Be *Authentic:* It takes too much energy to be someone or something that you are not; thus, it so much easier to be me, the real me, in every situation. However, I am still working on growing in this area.

Be *Teachable:* To learn is to lead and to lead is to constantly learn. The more teachable spirit I have, the better person I can become for myself, my family, friends, and my staff and students.

Grateful

With a renewed focus recently on mindfulness and social–emotional learning, there is mounting evidence that shows how displaying gratitude can have a positive impact on one's behavior and outlook. Some show gratitude by sending daily text messages to friends or family, sending personal notes, or making a gratitude list the first thing in the morning or the last thing before going to bed. Regardless of one's daily habit, it seems that those who take time to show gratitude have chosen to take control of their attitude, which, in turn, impacts their actions. The developers of *The Five-Minute Journal* (Ikonn and Ramdas, 2013) have created a tool that makes it easier for one to develop an attitude of gratitude. The developers state,

> *The Five Minute Journal* is created with leading positive psychology research. The Greater Good Science Center at the University of California, Davis, launched a multi-year project expanding the science and practice of gratitude. Here is what they found: "higher levels of positive emotion, more joy, optimism and happiness, feeling less

lonely and isolated, acting with more generosity and compassion, and stronger immune systems."
www.intelligentchange.com/pages/our-story

After experiencing some personal challenges this school year, a dear friend of mine gave me *The Five Minute Journal* and explained how it has helped her manage the stresses of life. Before using the journal, I thought I showed gratitude daily; however, the journal helped me to think more intentionally and deeply about the things of which I'm most thankful. I was able to focus more on the people in my life and the experiences I've been blessed to have, and the opportunities that have come my way.

I incorporated this practice into my weekly administrative team meetings by occasionally starting the meeting with each person stating what they are most thankful for. We all noticed how good we felt afterwards, and we began the week with a more positive outlook. To have a greater impact on our overall school culture, I also incorporated this into our department chair meetings by asking each department chair to share one thing about which they are most thankful. Many added this to their department meeting agendas as well. Those who shared their lists included some common things such as family, friends, sleep, rest, or good weather. Others were much more specific by commenting about a specific person, such as a colleague or student. These stories were impactful and helped to strengthen our school culture because they exemplified how our core values were exhibited in our work.

Great educators don't wait for an invitation, staff member, or centering activity to show gratitude; it's a skill or habit they take responsibility for and develop over time.

> Great educators don't wait for an invitation, staff member, or centering activity to show gratitude; it's a skill or habit they take responsibility for and develop over time.

Relational

Great educators understand that we need others. We understand that positive relationships are the foundation for significant learning to occur and for a positive culture to exist. When I was a student teacher, my advising professor commented on how I easily made connections with students and asked me how I did it. Unfortunately, I had no idea and simply said, "I don't know, it just happens." He pushed back quite a bit and asked me to think about what I did and to be more intentional as I started my teaching career. Twenty-four years later, I think I have an idea of how to create positive relationships but I'm always looking for ways to be better, as are most great educators!

The late great educator Rita Pierson said it best: "Kids don't learn from people they don't like." This also applies to the adult relationships in the school community: principal to staff, staff to staff, staff to parents, and principal to parents. In my experience, when the adults mistreat each other, there is an overall negative impact on student achievement and school culture. It is with that in mind that last school year, I partnered with leadership coach Jack Slavinski (from Lead4Influence) to facilitate personal skill development with my building leadership team (assistant principals and department chairs). Jack helped us respond with intention to the year-end culture survey data we gathered from staff. The data showed we needed to improve the adult relationships in the building beginning with my relationship with the teaching staff. I needed to continue to build trust or rebuild trust in some regard, but I didn't have a clear idea about how to do that until I spent some time with Jack. We started with an essential question: "What is trust and how do you build it?"

Jack outlined three fundamental disciplines one needs to establish trust: Connection, Character, and Competence. *Character* is ethical trust, and it's built primarily by being a person of your word, following through on your commitments and intentions, and being responsive to others. Character trust takes a great deal of time to earn and only a second to destroy. When we are intentional about establishing positive relationships like great educators should, we judge ourselves by our actions, not our intentions. *Connection* is personal trust. We build personal trust by caring deeply for others, by listening intently, and by flexing our personal style to meet the needs of others. *Competence* is technical trust, which is established by the experience we create for others in our care. It's built by solving problems with and for others, and by creating the conditions for others to experience success and contribute to the greater good of the school. All three disciplines of trust are equally important and lacking in one means there is an overall lack of trust. Period.

Great educators understand that trust is the foundation of strong relationships and strong relationships are the cornerstone of a positive classroom and school culture. Great educators also understand that we must know who we are and how we best connect with others by becoming a student of ourselves. For example, while working with Jack, each of us completed two important assessments:

> Great educators understand that we must know who we are and how we best connect with others by becoming a student of ourselves.

◆ The DISC Personality Assessment: www.123test.com/ disc-personality-test/
◆ The VIA Institute on Character Survey: www.viacharacter. org/survey/account/register

As we took the surveys and shared our results with each other, we became much closer, more understanding, and much more patient as we worked collaboratively to lead our school. Our dialogue was much more effective, and we developed deeper empathy for each other. We used scientifically proven research to support our need and desire to improve the adult relationships in our building so that we can improve the developmental outcomes of all our students. Following is an email from a department chair who incorporated these assessments in her department meetings in order to create the conditions for her team to become more collaborative:

Yesterday, my department colleagues completed the character strength survey, and today we discussed our results. Here are the questions I used to guide our discussion:

- *Are you surprised with your results? Why or why not?*
- *What (if any) patterns do you notice about our top character strengths as a department?*

- *How does being aware of your own character strengths benefit your teaching role?*
- *How might being aware of each other's character strengths benefit our department?*
- *What character signature trait are you going to purposefully use in the coming days or week?*

Three of the nine department members had "appreciation of beauty and excellence" as their top strength which surprised me since I do not remember that specific strength coming up much in our department chair meeting discussion. Everyone participated in the discussion, and many related these results back to the DISC personality survey we took earlier in the school year.

As you can tell, this exercise led to a great deal of personal and department reflection. As a result, the staff were more connected, felt more valued and respected, and were able to collaborate more intentionally to improve student learning.

As I stated earlier, we received some harsh feedback from our year-end climate survey. We used the data to refocus our efforts on three main areas: Connecting with others; providing clear and consistent communication; and making fewer mistakes and changes. I eliminated my weekly blogs and started meeting with teachers more often to strengthen personal trust (*connection*). For example: I scheduled a weekly meeting with the chairs of the departments I evaluate; I reduced the number of staff meetings in exchange for more department meeting times; and I scheduled monthly "Appy Hours" where one department a month was invited to attend a local restaurant for appetizers and conversation. These were well-received and much appreciated by staff and faculty.

I also established a Climate and Culture Committee that included several staff members, students, and parents. The objectives of the committee were:

- ◆ To understand the definitions and differences between school climate and school culture.
- ◆ To include stakeholders in the process to identify strengths and areas for improvement in regard to school climate and school culture.

◆ To identify two areas of focus for the 2017–2018 school year and develop an action plan.

◆ To develop outcomes to measure the success of our school climate and culture.

To strengthen personal character trust, I continued to deliver the daily Words of Wisdom (www.projectwisdom.com) because of the positive messages and opportunity to inspire students. I believe it is critical that students and staff hear from the principal every day. Project Wisdom also provides lesson plans and writing prompts for each message, so I shared them with teachers who asked for ways to incorporate the messages into their lessons for class discussions.

Several years ago, I had the chance to hear "The Freedom Writer," Erin Gruwell, speak about the power of relationships and she was on point! She shared her amazing story about how she worked with 150 challenging students to completely transform their lives. It was apparent that she really got to know her students, connected with them on a highly emotional level, and created a collaborative, safe learning environment for them to succeed. Her story was a reminder that mentoring relationships are messy. It's hard work and there are many obstacles to overcome. However, if the goal is to significantly impact the life of another person, then it's worth it.

Erin used the art of writing to tear down walls and open doors for students. Her story reminded me of a Challenge Day activity called, "Cross the Line." This activity helps participants find common ground and it provides a visual of how connected we truly are by shared experiences. We held a Challenge Day at my school several years ago and it did wonders for enhancing a positive school climate. Students, parents, staff, and community members still talk about how Challenge Day transformed their lives.

Listening to Erin's story and watching brief clips from the movie, *Freedom Writers*, reminded me of Todd Whitaker's phrase, "It's people, not programs." We all have an "Erin Gruwell" experience with students. We are reminded of these stories when we refer to the letters from former students that we receive. If you don't keep a file of these letters or cards, then I strongly encourage you to start today! We all have that one success story that brings tears to our eyes when we think about how we've made a difference to someone.

I recently ran into a former athlete I coached, who is now 29 years old and doing extremely well. He pulled me aside to talk. He said,

> You may not remember this, but when I was a freshman [he was a starter on the Varsity football team as a freshman], you walked up to me and told me I should run track because it would humble me. You said I hadn't experienced loss yet, but running track would help me grow as a person and understand humility. I never forgot that and I thank you for caring enough to tell me.

He was an extremely gifted athlete, he was charismatic, and he was a natural leader. I had noticed how he interacted with some of his peers in the hallways or on the field and was a bit concerned. I wasn't his specific position coach, but we had a close enough relationship where I thought he would be receptive. Thirteen years later, I had the rare encounter that allowed me to see that the positive relationship I had formed with him made a difference in how his character would form.

Each school year, my goal is to re-establish positive relationships with members of my staff. At times, I've allowed "programs" or other excuses to get in the way of relationships. To steal a phrase from Seth Godin (2018), as educators, "We have a platform to share our art." Our "art" is making a difference in the lives of others. Let's remember to use our platform (classroom, school building, cafeteria, front desk, attendance office, or guidance office) to establish significant relationships with others, set high expectations, and make a difference, more specifically, a positive difference, in someone's life.

Enthusiastic

With the divisive and combative culture in which we live right now, it can be challenging to be enthusiastic about our craft, but great educators know the only two things we can control are our attitudes and actions. Despite knowing this, being able to do something about it is not always easy. When great educators have an attitude of gratitude and focus on establishing positive relationships, then it's a little easier to be enthusiastic.

Whenever I found myself less than enthusiastic about my role as a school leader, I would create a chart: On the top left side of the chart, I would write the following question, "What am I most enthused about in my current role?" On the top right side of the chart I would write, "What am I least enthused about in my current role?" After completing this activity, I asked myself which of the things I could control. Inevitably, the list would include several things over which I had no control, which helped me to refocus on changing my actions in those areas I could control. For example, I would visit classrooms. It is energizing to be around students and teachers while they are in their element in the classroom. I enjoyed interacting with the students and observing quality instruction. Plus, it reminded me why I became an educator and my enthusiasm levels would increase.

My intent was to create the conditions for all students and staff to have a sense of belonging, and that began during our Back-to-School event and on the first day of school. The night before the first day of school, I partnered with a local balloon company and they would deliver 8–10 balloon towers and three large balloon arches. The arches were placed at each entrance and the towers lined the lobby area to create a fun, festive, and welcoming environment. We also played popular (school-appropriate) music over the PA system to let students know we were excited and enthused to begin the school year! We also rented a few large air men and displayed them in our drop off loop! The parents loved to see these large figures flopping and waving as they brought their children to school. The first day of school comes once each year, so why not treat it like a day of celebration, setting a positive tone from the start?

Great educators understand the importance of an enthusiastic attitude and realize it's all about mindset. Educators are busy and have long to-do lists each day. These lists can

> Great educators understand the importance of an enthusiastic attitude and realize it's all about mindset.

also deter us from giving our best each day and we may tend to feel like we "need to" or "have to" take attendance, call parents, respond to emails, create lesson plans, etc. But great educators say,

- ◆ I get to take attendance!
- ◆ I choose to call parents!
- ◆ I get to respond to emails!
- ◆ I choose to create meaningful lesson plans!

By simply changing the wording from "I have to" to "I get to," great educators demonstrate what it's like to have a positive attitude.

One of my favorite videos to watch is about a blind man sitting on the ground with a cardboard sign next to him that reads, "I'M BLIND PLEASE HELP." The ground is damp under cloudy skies and the man is patiently sitting with his arms crossed and not saying much to anyone. Several people walk by him without even a glance, while others drop a few coins at his feet. One young lady, as she walks past him, takes a second to read his sign. She stops, picks up his sign, pulls out a black marker from her coat, scribbles something on his sign, puts the sign back down and walks off. Soon after, nearly everyone who walks past the man drops coins and dollars at his feet! The man is completely overwhelmed by it. He has a keen sense of hearing and notices the sound of the young lady's footsteps as she returns. She stops and stands in front of him; he reaches out to touch her shoes, turns his face toward hers and asks, "What did you do with my sign?" She kneels down in front of him, touches him on the shoulder and says, "I wrote the same, but different words." The sign she created read, "IT'S A BEAUTIFUL DAY AND I CAN'T SEE IT." The moral of the story:

Change your words, change your world.

Combining an attitude of gratitude, an understanding of the importance of establishing positive and trusting relationships, and enthusiasm to do great work, educators can indeed change other's worlds too!

Authentic

Ralph Waldo Emerson said it best: "To be yourself in a world that is constantly trying to make you something else is the greatest accomplishment." As great educators innovate their practice by focusing on personal skill development, we understand the need to become the very best version of ourselves each day. It's no secret that expectations of educators have increased exponentially over the years and we may oftentimes struggle to be our true selves as a result of the pressure that comes with increased expectations.

This is probably the one discipline that I struggle with the most. I noticed over the years that the more people for whom I was responsible, the less authentic I became. I'm not sure if it was a matter of self-preservation, protection, or fatigue but I found myself exhausted by the end of the day mainly because I tried hard to maintain a perception of "having it all together." What has helped me overcome this are the results I received from the VIA Character Survey (www.viacharacter.org/survey/account/register) and the DISC Personality Test (www.123test.com/disc-personality-test/) that I have previously mentioned.

The VIA Character Survey assesses one's strength in 24 scientifically identified characteristics. It is comprised of over 100 questions for the user to answer and at the end it provides a detailed report that ranks one's characteristics from 1 to 24. It is important to point out that the results are not to be read as "strengths versus weaknesses" but it identifies which characteristics are most dominant compared to which ones are less dominant. Once I was equipped with this information, I was able to reflect on the way I lead as a principal and my daily mindset. It was enlightening to say the least and gave me a fresh perspective of myself, how I view others, and how my daily actions aligned with my core beliefs or steered away from them. As a result, I started to enjoy my days even more and had a renewed clarity about what I wanted to accomplish personally and professionally.

The DISC Personality Test provided even more clarity for me in regard to my leadership style, how I interact with others, and how I respond. Authenticity has helped me to better support my students, staff, and administrative team because I am able to demonstrate that I care deeply for them (*responsiveness*), provide more intentional help (*supportive*), and flex my leadership style to meet their needs (*adaptability*). Great educators know that students can tell if you are being authentic or a fraud. They know if you are sincere or if you are sinister. They know if you can be trusted. They can tell, and they want authenticity from the educators who have been entrusted to care for and about them. The author Iain Thomas summarized it best when he said, "Someone you haven't even met yet is wondering what it'd be like to know someone like you." Be authentically you!

> Great educators know that students can tell if you are being authentic or a fraud. They know if you are sincere or if you are sinister. They know if you can be trusted.

Teachable

There's an old Jewish proverb that states, "Before the fall is pride." Those who are proud lack a teachable or coachable spirit. To innovate personal skill development, great educators remain open to learning more about themselves, others, and how to improve our craft. There is pride in the work we do but not "puffed up" or arrogant pride that prevents growth from taking place. In this era of rapid change and a number of disruptions, having a teachable spirit or mindset is a necessity for success.

In the last few years, I've had the opportunity to present at several conferences or workshops about how I use social media to tell our school's story. Each time that I share examples, tell stories, and start with our "why," I notice two different responses:

♦ Arms crossed, furrowed brow, and a blank stare as if to say, "This will never work in my school or district."
♦ Pen frantically scribbling across the paper, head nodding in agreement, and hands raised with questions.

I get it. I've had both reactions. But I have come to embrace, promote, encourage, and model the use of social media, in which

I share stories, highlight staff, make connections, and engage in the learning process through "chats."

Inevitably, I am approached by teachers at the end of each session who ask: "How do I get my administration to allow mobile devices at school or to embrace the use of social media?" The look of despair in their eyes reminds me that while many educators across the globe use social media and Web 2.0 tools to increase learning opportunities, connect with others, engage learners, and share information, there are far too many who are still reluctant or resistant to it altogether. Change is difficult, especially when it comes to changing a mindset. However, we must continue to share successful stories of how teachers and students are using social media to positively change lives and impact futures. We can start by looking within our own building. We can then promote what other educators and students are doing from other districts. The more we share, the better the chance we have of turning reluctance and resistance into openness and acceptance.

We must also become keenly aware of the disruptions educators face today. The more aware we are of these disruptions, the better able we will be to adapt to the changes with which we are faced. This cannot occur if we are not teachable. You would be hard pressed to talk to a teacher, secretary, or school administrator who would say we are not experiencing some disruptive times in education. Since 2008, public perception of educators, in general, has been less than favorable. Expectations have increased exponentially, yet funding education initiatives have not grown at the same pace. One might say we face one disruption after another, yet we continue to find ways to meet the needs of our students, engage parents, respond to community desires, and do what is best for all stakeholders.

I recently co-authored *Leading Schools in Disruptive Times: How to Survive Hyper-Change* with my mentor and good friend Mark White (Carter and White, 2017). As the political and social climate in our nation has changed, the release of this book could not have come at a better time. With that in mind, we describe seven disruptions school leaders face today:

Student Safety: School safety has taken on a whole new meaning since Columbine. Greater measures are in place to identify students who do not feel a sense of belonging and society continues to grapple with how to reduce and eliminate school shootings. Schools are asked to provide in-depth mental health supports while focusing on the academic progress and achievement of students.

Accelerating Technology: Technology has become cheaper, smaller, faster, and more accessible than ever before and school leaders must find ways to integrate its use in schools.

Reform Efforts: Unfunded and rapidly changing mandates that include new ways of assessing student learning to more complex evaluation systems leave school leaders scrambling to keep up.

Generational Challenges: Millennials are entering the teaching ranks that are led by Gen X'ers and Boomers. Without an adaptive mindset, this could negatively impact overall student achievement if not handled properly.

Global Readiness: Skill development is far more important than content absorption, so school leaders have to work with stakeholders to define what success looks like in their schools and identify the key skills they want students to develop.

Complex Diversity Issues: Race, gender, immigration, and sexual identity are topics that create diversity challenges for today's school leaders.

Demand for Transparency: Information is accessible 24/7 and stakeholders demand that school leaders find ways to keep them informed about student performance, provide report card data, and immediately provide safety updates at a moment's notice. It's become a societal expectation.

This may seem overwhelming, and it is. However, having a teachable attitude or spirit can help great educators navigate the ways of change! In such a time as this, former principal, assistant superintendent, and superintendent Mark White says,

It's often the administrator's voice that must resonate. In dark times, it must be a ray of light that others may follow. Now more than ever, administrators must be visible and plugged in with their students and staff.

Being "GREAT"

To be GREAT is more than just a catchy acronym. It is a way to focus our intentions on serving others in a way that influences their lives in a positive manner. Great educators are aware that the attitude we bring to the table and our actions really do make a difference and the only barrier that may truly stand in our way is the person in the mirror. That same person has the power to create the conditions for us to Be GREAT!

References

Carter, D. L. and White, M. E. (2017). *Leading Schools in Disruptive Times: How to Survive Hyper-Change.* Thousand Oaks, CA: Corwin.

Godin, S. (2018). *Linchpin: Are You Indispensable? How to Drive Your Career and Create a Remarkable Future.* London: Piatkus.

Ikonn, A. and Ramdas, U. J. (2013). *The Five Minute Journal: A Happier You in 5 Minutes a Day.* Toronto: Intelligent Change.

10

Taking Risks and Pushing Boundaries

LaVonna Roth

Miss, you have to make this happen. You have to. – Devon, grade 12

A few years ago, I sat with seven high school seniors around a small table in a conference room to discuss their next steps in life. They were graduating in three weeks. These students were defying the odds as some of them were about to be the first in their family to graduate from high school. Many of them had already faced things in life that many of us adults would have trouble handling. Although their backgrounds and their circumstances caused me to have empathy for them, it was their words that caused a rush of frustration and a waterfall of emotion that poured over me as I listened during one particular point in the conversation.

I had just asked them to tell me about their strengths; what they were good at in school. The room went silent. They uncomfortably looked at each other and wiggled in their seats uneasily. At first, I thought perhaps it was because they were uncomfortable with sharing out loud something positive about themselves in front of their peers; particularly fearful of being laughed at or concerned that they would appear arrogant. However, that was not to be the primary reason. As they looked at each other, one student finally spoke. "My strengths?" he asked, turning to look me in the eyes. I said, "Yes. What are those things in school that are your strengths, gifts, skills, or talents?" The stares continued in my direction. More silence. What they proceeded to share thereafter was all of their weaknesses. I had to fight tears at that moment because I realized what we had done. In education our focus is so much on what students *can't do*, that we forget to show them (and celebrate) what they *can do*. Great educators focus on both. They focus on helping students understand their weaknesses and to improve in those areas, but great educators also know that a student's strengths will propel them further in life, because that is where their passion comes from and what will drive them to succeed. As an educator of 22 years, I am disheartened by our constant focus on testing and our lack of focus on the whole child and serving that person.

> In education our focus is so much on what students *can't do*, that we forget to show them (and celebrate) what they *can do*. Great educators focus on both.

As a lifelong educator in a variety of roles, I have come to embrace some "best practices" in education while at the same time questioning some other "best practices." Throughout much of my childhood and adulthood, I was taught to not question authority or the way things are. They are as they are for a reason and I was to abide by that. Yet, a voice inside me began like a flicker when I started my career as a teacher, questioning some of the so-called "best practices" in education. That flicker has become a much larger flame, a voice, like trying to hold back a volcano. This volcanic emotion has given me the burning desire to not only raise awareness regarding what truly is fair, but also to help create change that no longer accepts things for as they are. That voice inside me can no longer stay quiet because it is not my place to speak up or for fear of repercussions. It is my place. It is your place. We are all responsible for every child. When we sit in silence or chat quietly with each other, we are not creating a solution, but rather allowing things to remain the same. It is time. Time to speak out, take risks for students, and push boundaries that need to be pushed. It is time to stop shoving students into a box known as the educational system, but rather to teach so the educational system fits the student.

In some ways, it is a simple shift. If we approach teaching through the lens of the child, the shift is easier. We teach the individual instead of the norm. For example, if a child loves to dance, we could have them model Newton's Third Law of Motion through dance moves. If a child is challenged by a math concept of numbers greater than another number and loves football, we could use the football field as an example number line. By teaching in this manner, we begin to honor and value the individual, supporting who they are and what they can become.

More Than Just Words, We Must Do

In Ignite Your S.H.I.N.E.®, a movement I started back in 2015, we focus on the five components of S.H.I.N.E. to assist educators in creating a way of "being" – as opposed to following a program – in their classroom, school, or district. The letters of S.H.I.N.E. stand for: *Self, Heart, Inspire, Navigate*, and *Exceptional*.

The first two letters signify how to reach and teach students with what you want them to learn while honoring and valuing who they are. *Self* focuses on strengths, gifts, skills, and talents, along with mindsets, social–emotional well-being and perseverance. *Heart* is the core of passion and purpose. When we teach students using their strengths (over their weaknesses) and using their passions as examples, we will reach them and they will learn like never before. Imagine the love of learning and excitement of coming to school in knowing that each student recognizes that they have areas of weakness, yet they also have strengths. Strengths lead to opportunities for success. Success builds confidence. Confidence is what we need to build so our students do not feel the need to bully other students to try to feel better, so they can take feedback without offense, and so they can be productive, healthy citizens who are willing to take risks. I say the latter about students, but

> When we teach students using their strengths (over their weaknesses) and using their passions as examples, we will reach them and they will learn like never before.

it also applies to educators. In a world where we compare ourselves to each other and to the average, we set up a danger zone.

As humans, that is what we do. We compare. We measure ourselves to one another. I find how and what we compare interesting. What often happens is that we see one person who has a strength in one area and another person in another area and so on, and we often compare from a perspective of feeling we don't do any of those things well or as well. What we need to realize is that not one person has all of those things and does all of them well, yet it's easy for us to feel that we are not as good as them or that we are not enough. Taking the approach through the lens of knowing that we all have strengths to offer shifts the approach to one of comparing without harsh self-judgment since we all have gifts to contribute.

Unfortunately, our education system is still designed for average students to fit into the model from a time when we needed people to work in factories. Who would be good at a desk job? Who would find success on the factory floor? Who fits a managerial role? Due to this factory model, our schools have resulted in bells ringing (the start and end to a factory shift) and rows for learning (the assembly lines or desk job in a factory). For me, I chose to earn both of my Masters degrees specifically from universities that did not require me to take a test. Both of them had me prove what I knew through a portfolio; a demonstration of my knowledge. Yet, we measure students according to a test and we average grades together to compare students and tell them where they stand among their peers.

High school dropout Todd Rose (2017, p.8) believes:

Any system designed around the average person is doomed to fail.

We cannot afford to fail our students. Yet each time we show a lack of empathy to students for the challenges they face and every time we do not adjust our teaching to meet their social–emotional needs first, we miss an opportunity to put their brain into a state of learning so they can be successful. Successful in school and life. These opportunities help students to see how we handle challenges. We provide a window of opportunity by being vulnerable so students can see how challenges can be a way to teach us a life lesson, or give us an opportunity to draw strength from, for future events.

When students compare themselves to the average, we either provide an opportunity to elevate, stay the same, or digress. I would rather provide students with a model of elevation, always. Great educators assist in elevation by showing empathy to students and the situation, then sitting with them to discover what strength can come from what happened. It is why I am a fan of students not being successful at times early in life. If they do not have an opportunity to fail or be challenged, there will be a time or many in their lives when they will experience such things and be uncertain as to how to handle it. As students grow up, we can rise to the opportunity to help them see what good can come from a lesson learned and be shown how to elevate in such circumstances.

I remember when one of my grade 2 students, Charlie, had so much anger that he did not know how to control the emotion. He would let the anger out by throwing chairs in the classroom, shoving desks, and clenching his fists and teeth with a growling sound. After several outbursts, I realized the issue. I decided to try an idea I had found in a magazine. I set up a table in the reading center with plain white copy paper and crayons. When Charlie came in the next morning, I talked with him about how sometimes we all get angry and it can be hard to know what to do and how to handle that anger. I shared times with him when I had felt angry and how it is okay to be angry, but it is not okay to let the anger out however we want. This was us sharing together and relating to the frustration of having these strong emotions. It was in that moment that we bonded even more because he realized he was not alone and I realized he was a young human trying to cope with things that we even have trouble handling as adults. I then showed him the table in the reading center. His eyes widened as I modeled what the paper and crayons were for. They were for every time Charlie felt anger rising, he was to come to the table and color as hard and as fast as he could. If a crayon broke, he was to grab another. If the paper was covered, he was to grab another sheet. Charlie only had to do this twice before he began to recognize when his anger was welling. That was a day of progress; getting him to realize when he was becoming angry was a first step.

By the way, author Todd Rose, mentioned earlier, now serves as the Director of the Mind, Brain and Education program at the Harvard Graduate School of Education.

Taking a Stand for Students

In order to set students up for success in life, we have to address some of the current situations in schools. Currently, our education system awards and recognizes those who are good test takers. Most schools are set up to provide students with a grade that reflects a student's learning – but this is faulty. Imagine that I am going to take you for your driver's test to get your license for the very first time and you have never driven a car. In class, I showed you movies about how to drive and had you practice identifying where the brake pedal and gas pedal are, so I believe that you should be able to drive successfully. If this were a real situation, how successful would you be? Not very. Why? Because you did not have opportunities to practice and experience what it means to actually drive a car. Imagine I had taken a grade every time you practiced driving in the classroom. Would your performance be a true reflection of what you are able to do while actually driving the car? Absolutely not. However, we do this to students all day every day. We take grades on learning components and average them together with the final performance as if that truly reflects the learning. If they learned to drive really well by the end, the final grade would not be a reflection of the true learning. A pop quiz, a test that covers more than what was taught, or even simply the fact that it's a test, is not a true reflection of what has been learned and what the student can do with that information.

Not only do we take grades on the practices, but the majority of the assessments are paper–pencil tests. What that means is: our assessments are geared toward those who take tests well. As a matter of fact, we often label students who do well in school paper–pencil tests as "smart." Why is the unit of measure for knowledge and being "smart" a paper–pencil test? Out of all the job opportunities out there, how many of them, realistically, require someone to take a paper–pencil test? There may be some, but I am confident that if we created a random list of 100 jobs, very few would require a test. So we have a system, in theory, set up for, perhaps, 25% of jobs. What about the other 75%?

Let's play devil's advocate and say that all jobs require a test in order to be hired: 100% of them. An individual takes the test and gets the job. Let's say they change jobs every three years and work until they are 60 years old, having started working at the age of 16. That is 44 years of work. Since they are taking a test for every job, every three years, that's 15 tests they will take over 44 years. Our school system has prepped them to take tests, so they are ready for them; but what about all the other days they are not taking a test and instead are applying, learning, creating, innovating, negotiating, communicating, and problem solving? There are 16,060 days in 44 years of work. Taking 15 tests equals 15 days out of 16,060 days total. Obviously, this is an extreme example, yet it drives home the point that the amount of test prep and test taking students do in school is not what sets them up for success in life. You can take a test and get the job, but if that is where skill set and work ethic stop, that person will not have the job for long.

We do a disservice when we gear our system toward testing. Our students take a test to be promoted to the next grade level, to graduate, to get into college and out. After that, some jobs may require an application test, but very few in the overall scheme of how many jobs are out there, and especially those that are now being created. May I remind you that those paper–pencil tests compare students to … the average. It is time we change a system that does not match the real world and does not do what is best for students. This is easy to say, but harder to do. It is not hopeless though and it can be done for our children. We start with using our voices and making any small changes we can, and we start

> It is time we change a system that does not match the real world and does not do what is best for students.

to push boundaries through conversations with stakeholders. It is possible and it will take educators like you to stand up for our students along with giving parents and students a voice.

Moving Away from the Traditional

Once we take tests out of the equation, averaging stops. It becomes about the individual. Universities are coming on board with this notion, too. Georgia Institute of Technology, MIT, Duke University, and University of Berkeley, California, are just a few that are providing credential opportunities (www.class-central. com/certificate). These opportunities allow an individual to take courses of interest in a particular field to build a résumé of uniqueness. Companies hire the individual based on what that person has and may ask them to earn some other select credentials that they want them to have based upon the individual needs of that company. Rather than having a cookie cutter four-year degree, like everyone else, companies are able to hire applicants based on the needs of their company.

Just as every student is not a test taker, some would not be successful at a traditional college or university – nor may it be necessary for them to go. Let's take a look at traditional higher education at colleges and universities. As mentioned before, many individuals walk out with a cookie cutter degree. Not that this is necessarily bad since there are certain components necessary for some careers. However, our world is shifting and companies are moving very quickly toward innovation and implementation of ideas. Barriers to traditional thinking and practices are being broken, as seen by companies such as Lyft and Airbnb. The list is quickly growing and will continue to do so. There is so much choice. Think about companies such as Starbucks® that helped break the mold of ordering your drink exactly how you want it. At one point, my order at Starbucks® was a "tall, non-fat, no whip, mocha, with 2 pumps and extra hot" (yes, I was that person). We live in a time where individualism is catered to and is becoming the expected. This makes me wonder if getting a degree is actually the right push.

According to the National Center for Education Statistics in the U.S. (2018), 19.9 million students attended American colleges and universities in fall 2018. Yet the Bureau of Labor Statistics (2014) reports that "only about one-third of all jobs require education beyond high school." Only one-third. Don't misunderstand me. I do believe there is a need for higher education and that more skill sets and experiences come from attending college than pure academia, but other possibilities of professional pathways should be looked at with equal weight. When the U.S. Bureau of Census reports that, in 2010, only 27.3% of college graduates hold a job that is similar to the major they earned (Plumer, 2013), and we consider that these college graduates are buried under a debt of tens to hundreds of thousands of dollars, we owe it to them to determine if going to college is the best option.

I know for me, going to college was the expectation. It never even crossed my mind to not go. So I would like to see options shared with every student so they can make a more informed choice rather than saying you must go to college to be successful (as defined by "them" – i.e., prestige, finances, lifestyle, etc.). A choice where they have been exposed to multiple fields and multiple career paths. One company that has started to help students to get exposed to career paths is Thrively. Students can discover their strengths and interests through online surveys, videos, and local hands-on experiences. By doing so, students receive better direction as to which path may be more in line with who they are and what they want to do in life. They have a chance to understand more of what is out there and available to them, beyond the current world of what they know.

At a higher education level, Adam Braun started MissionU, a college alternative, where individuals commit to one year of learning through real-world experiences with no money up front to start. Classes are taught by top industry leaders, those who are currently in the field. Tuition is paid after you graduate and there is a commitment to help you find a job, unlike traditional universities where you are handed a piece of paper and they owe you nothing – but you sure owe them! By the way, did you know that, according to Complete College America (2018), only 19% of college students earn a degree in four years? Do the math on that one! MissionU's website stated,

> we're interested in how you think and what you're capable of, not what score you got on a standardized test.
>
> www.missionu.com (July 2018)

Adam and MissionU understand that how a student performs on a test does not determine their success in life.

More traditional universities are starting to agree. The Making Caring Common Project by Harvard Graduate School of Education outlines multiple goals needed to reshape the college admissions process to promote the "common good" in the hope of "promoting and assessing ethical and intellectual engagement" (2016, p.4). The process is no longer based heavily on the sole SAT or ACT score; it now includes how and whether students can work "effectively and sensitively with those who are different from them in background or other characteristics" (Harvard Graduate School of Education, 2016, p.19). The project even goes as far as to encourage universities and colleges to make these tests optional. It is worth noting that there are currently 66 universities which have endorsed this project's goals and have already begun addressing some admissions changes.

Becoming an Illuminator

Shifts have begun at various levels of higher education and in industries. The question of why we are doing things the way they have always been has come to light. As educators, we too must start considering this. Taking a closer look at policies and "best practices" will help us fine-tune what our gut and heart have often told us. In various fields, people have taken the average of something and created a baseline for that average. Time and time again, the average has proven faulty because it does not represent the individual, but rather a conglomerate of a lot of data. Data that combined has one representation, but when compared to each individual person, it represents no one. Data is useful, but if the data represents an average, is it really an accurate representation of where we want our students to be?

As I reflect back on sitting with those seven seniors a few years back, I am struck by the words that one student said to me. I had just shared my vision for a school that embraces students' strengths and passions as a driving force in learning, that builds up confidence on a daily basis, where students can experience career opportunities before they graduate so they are exposed to possibilities, and schools where innovation of thoughts and ideas are permitted to be tried. As I continued sharing with them my vision, Devon, a student, turned and looked me in the eyes and said, "Miss, you have to make this happen. You have to." I looked down and said, "I'm not sure how to make it happen financially because it will take a lot of money and help." As he looked me in the eyes, again, he whispered, "Where there's a will there's a way. You can do this." Wow. It was in that moment that I knew I could no longer stay silent on what needed to change. The best part is – I don't have to do this alone. Nor do I want to do this alone. It will take each and every great educator to take a stand in doing what is best for students by taking risks and pushing boundaries. For that, I invite you to become an *Illuminator*.

An illuminator is someone who focuses on helping individuals discover their greatness and helps them understand how to illuminate the world with that greatness. An illuminator isn't fearful of having tough conversations that may involve a difference of opinion, but has what is best for students at the heart of every decision. An illuminator creates opportunities for students to explore and discover who they are by providing opportunities outside of the content, and in some cases, outside of the academia box. An illuminator seeks out chances to help students through learning opportunities that come from mistakes, failed plans, or negativity from others. An illuminator understands that empathy is a key to positive relationships, and positive relationships are the key to supporting students for school and lifelong success.

> To professionally challenge the way things have always been done and not silently accepting certain policies or paths can be tough, but the right change does not always come from making easy decisions.

I know what I am asking. To professionally challenge the way things have always been done and not silently accepting certain policies or paths can be tough, but the right change does not always come from making easy decisions. If we chose education because we care about students, then we must take a vocal and actionable stand in this urgent matter. It is asking a school system to recognize and honor our children for their strengths and passions; the whole child. It is asking for us to break down the box of confinement and comparison and rather to see each child for who they are and who they can be. It can be done. It must be done. They deserve it.

References

Bureau of Labor Statistics. (2014). Education Level and Jobs: Opportunities by State. Accessed October 10, 2018: www.bls.gov/careeroutlook/2014/article/education-level-and-jobs.htm

Complete College America. (2018). American Dreams are Powered by College Completion. Accessed October 4, 2018: https://completecollege.org/

Harvard Graduate School of Education. (2016). Turning the Tide: Inspiring Concern for Others and the Common Good through College Admissions. Accessed October 4, 2018: https://mcc.gse.harvard.edu/collegeadmissions

National Center for Education Statistics. (2018). Fast Facts: Back to School Statistics. Accessed October 4, 2018: https://nces.ed.gov/fastfacts/display.asp?id=372

Plumer, B. (2013). Only 27 Percent of College Grads Have a Job Related to Their Major. Accessed October 8, 2018: www.washingtonpost.com/news/wonk/wp/2013/05/20/only-27-percent-of-college-grads-have-a-job-related-to-their-major/?noredirect=on&utm_term=.09fec9311c91

Rose, T. (2017). The End of Average: How to Succeed in a World that Values Sameness. London: Penguin.

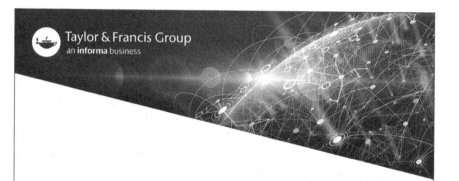